Museum of Anthropology
University of Michigan
Technical Reports
Number 17

RESEARCH REPORTS IN ARCHAEOLOGY
Contribution 12

Zooarchaeology of Six Prehistoric Sites in the Sierra Blanca Region, New Mexico

by

Jonathan C. Driver

with a foreword by John D. Speth

Ann Arbor
1985

Printed in the
United States of America

ISBN 0-915703-07-6

CONTENTS

LIST OF TABLES

LIST OF FIGURES

FOREWORD

Despite its vast area and its critical location along the interface between puebloan farmers to the west and nomadic hunters and gatherers to the east, southeastern New Mexico has received pitifully little attention from the archaeological profession. Neglect of the area is tragic because its fragile prehistoric record is rapidly vanishing in the face of energy development, urban expansion, vandalism, and other hallmarks of twentieth-century "progress." By the time archaeologists come to recognize the importance of southeastern New Mexico, there will be little left from which to piece together the area's fascinating culture history.

A major reason why archaeologists have ignored the area is its lack of monumental or picturesque sites, which elsewhere in the Southwest have become equated with archaeological "significance" or "importance." Southeastern New Mexico is often mistakenly dismissed as "marginal"; and, because of its supposed marginality, the area is assumed to be of little or no real importance for understanding puebloan developments in the "heartland" of the Southwest. An extension of this view, of course, is that the area's prehistory holds little or no potential for solving any problems of interest to anthropological archaeologists.

The tragedy of this position is that southeastern New Mexico offers unique opportunities for attacking some of the most interesting problems confronting the field today. An excellent example of the area's research potential is provided by the marginality issue itself. Southeastern New Mexico is anything but marginal, if by that term archaeologists have in mind an area unsuitable for horticulture. The area is characterized by considerable environmental diversity, with high mountains, deep protected canyons, rolling foothills and mesas, and broad lowlying valleys and basins. The rainfall in the area is variable, but the average is comparable to, or higher than the average amount that falls elsewhere in the Southwest. In many parts of southeastern New Mexico, the growing season is longer than on the Colorado Plateau, arable soils are more widespread, and surface water, prior to the drastic lowering of the watertable in the past century, was abundantly available in the Pecos and in several of its western tributaries. Southeastern New Mexico may have been peripheral to the rest of the Southwest, but it certainly was not marginal.

But if the unspectacular archaeological record of southeastern New Mexico is not due in some simple and direct way to restrictive environmental conditions, the absence of large-scale puebloan communities must be related to other, perhaps social, political, or economic, factors. Thus, rather than rendering the area uninteresting, this makes southeastern New Mexico an ideal natural laboratory for archaeological research aimed at exploring the full range of conditions, not merely the climatic ones, which underlie the development, success, or failure of horticultural communities in the Southwest.

Unfortunately, because so much of the region's archaeological record is already gone, materials excavated in the past and now housed in various American and Canadian museums become particularly precious resources. One of the most important of these earlier projects in southeastern New Mexico was a series of excavations conducted between 1950 and 1956 by Texas Technological College. The results of these excavations were written up in 1966 by Jane Holden Kelley as a Harvard University doctoral dissertation, but they remained largely inaccessible to the profession until their recent publication by the Museum of Anthropology of the University of Michigan (Kelley 1984). Kelley's study is a monumental work that presents invaluable data on the chronology, architecture, and material culture of several prehistoric communities in the Sacramento Mountain area, most of which no longer exist today. However, one critical facet of Kelley's analysis was never completed--a detailed study of the faunal remains. Fortunately, the recovery methods used in these early excavations were exemplary, and the collection of animal bones was carefully curated with the hope that it would someday be studied.

We are extremely fortunate that these remains have now been systematically analyzed by Jonathan Driver, and the results of his meticulous study are presented here. Driver's study clearly documents the range and proportions of hunted foods in the diet of the late prehistoric communities excavated by Kelley. It also contributes an interesting perspective to a growing discussion concerning the importance of local catchments versus community-level socioeconomic patterns in determining the diversity and modal body size of the animals that were hunted (Speth and Scott 1985). We are especially pleased to be able to publish Driver's data in full. This data base will provide an invaluable archaeological resource for many years to come. As our questions change and our understanding of the region's prehistory improves, archaeologists will be able to return repeatedly to these data and profitably rework them in new or different ways. Driver's study clearly demonstrates the tremendous research value of older faunal collections that now lie buried in the dim recesses of museums, and it adds a critical dimension to our understanding of the prehistory of southeastern New Mexico and the Southwest.

John D. Speth
Ann Arbor, Michigan
October 1985

ACKNOWLEDGMENTS

I would like to thank Jane Kelley for encouraging me to undertake this research and for providing financial assistance. John Speth has encouraged me to write a detailed report on the analyses, and his own research in the area has provided me with a greater stimulus than he probably realizes. I am also most grateful for his careful and critical reviews of this manuscript.

My research assistants were Rick Garvin, Norman Haywood, and Linda Gullason, all of whom I thank for their work in sorting and classifying bones.

Figures were prepared by Bryan Snow and by the Instructional Media Centre, Simon Fraser University. I am grateful to the Department of Archaeology, Simon Fraser University for funds to pay for the figures. The Dean of Arts Office, S.F.U., kindly supplied word processing services. Barbara Barnett typed all stages of the manuscript, including the final camera-ready copy. Publication was assisted by a generous grant from S.F.U.

Finally, many thanks to my family--Cathy, Simon, and Andrew--for accompanying me on the University of Calgary/Lakehead University field project in the Sierra Blanca region in 1984.

1
THE REGION AND THE SITES

Introduction

From 1950 to 1956 Dr. W. C. Holden of the Texas Technological College organized excavations at various sites in eastern New Mexico. A number of these excavations were supervised by J. H. Kelley, who subsequently wrote her Ph.D. dissertation on the later prehistory of the area west of Roswell, New Mexico, designated the Sierra Blanca region (Kelley 1966, 1984).

Holden and Kelley systematically collected faunal remains from the excavated sites, and these survived as a collection until the mid-1970s when Kelley began a re-study project of the area (Kelley 1979). The faunal remains were partially analyzed by Brian Kooyman, then an undergraduate at Calgary (Kooyman n.d.), and his results were reported briefly by Kelley (1979). Subsequently, Kelley obtained a grant from the University of Calgary to fund a more comprehensive study of the faunal remains, the preliminary results of which have been reported previously (Driver 1982, 1984a).

The aim of this paper is to provide a fuller documentation of the faunal remains from six sites, and to provide more discussion of the assemblages than has been undertaken so far. This paper is the final report of my work on these assemblages. In it I provide a brief description of the Sierra Blanca region and its later prehistory. I then discuss the methodology of data generation, presentation, and analysis. Finally, the six assemblages are discussed, and inter-site comparisons made.

The Region

The Sierra Blanca region extends east from the peaks of the Sacramento and Sierra Blanca ranges to the western boundary of the Pecos Valley, with northern and southern boundaries defined by the Gallo and Penasco drainages respectively (Fig. 1). Relief is varied. The major ranges in the west consist of Permian San Andres limestone which dips steeply towards the Pecos Valley. The limestone is partially mantled by Quaternary alluvial deposits, and dissected by various arroyo systems. This sedimentary system is interrupted in places by laccoliths, the most notable being Capitan Mountain, and by volcanic peaks such as Carrizo (Kelley 1966:47-48).

Today the region is characterized by Upper Sonoran vegetation from the foothills to the edge of the Pecos Valley. The upper limits of this zone include the piñon-juniper belt where many prehistoric villages were located to take advantage of the arable combination of alluvium and water. Most precipitation falling on the mountains fails to reach the Pecos through surface drainage, although permanent water is present in the Rio Hondo and Rio Penasco. As will be seen, faunal evidence shows that these were permanent watercourses during the prehistoric occupation of the area. Above the Upper Sonoran zone, Transitional and Canadian vegetation types can be found in the mountains, but few sites occur in these zones (Kelley 1966:48-49).

Prehistory

The prehistory of the Jornada Mogollon area has been summarized recently by Wiseman (1983), who retains Kelley's (1966) phases for the Sierra Blanca region. The archaeology of the region prior to about A.D. 1100 is poorly known, but presumably included an Archaic followed by an undefined ceramic period. At about A.D. 1100 the Glencoe Phase began in the southern part of the Sierra Blanca region, and lasted until about A.D. 1450 To the north, two phases span the same time period: Corona (1100-1200) and Lincoln (1200-1450). For the three phases sedentary or semi-sedentary villages are known, and agriculture was definitely practiced. The Glencoe Phase villages were characteristically clusters of pithouses, although in the late Glencoe manifestation at the Bonnell site pithouses were arranged to form multi-room units, apparently in imitation of the pueblo style (Kelley 1966:61).

In the Corona Phase, contemporary with early Glencoe to the south, villages consisted of scattered pithouses outlined with upright slabs, and presumably with a jacal superstructure (Kelley 1966:66). The succeeding Lincoln Phase contains the only examples of stone and adobe multi-roomed pueblos in the region. However, this architecture is not universal, and single adobe rooms are combined with pithouses at some sites (Kelley 1966:69). Subterranean ceremonial structures were also identified.

Kelley suggests that the Sierra Blanca region was largely abandoned by A.D. 1450, because Glaze II and III pottery is absent. However, recent reconsideration of the time span of Glaze I products (Cordell and Earls 1984) shows that occupation could have continued later than A.D. 1450 As yet the date of abandonment is unresolved.

The Sites

Faunal assemblages from six sites are discussed in this paper (Fig. 1). The Bonnell site is the major excavated site of the Glencoe Phase. The faunal sample was recovered from 33 excavated pithouses and surface jacal rooms. The site lies close to the Rio Ruidoso, on a terrace remnant to the north of the river. The permanent watercourse allows cottonwood and walnut trees to grow in the valley, although

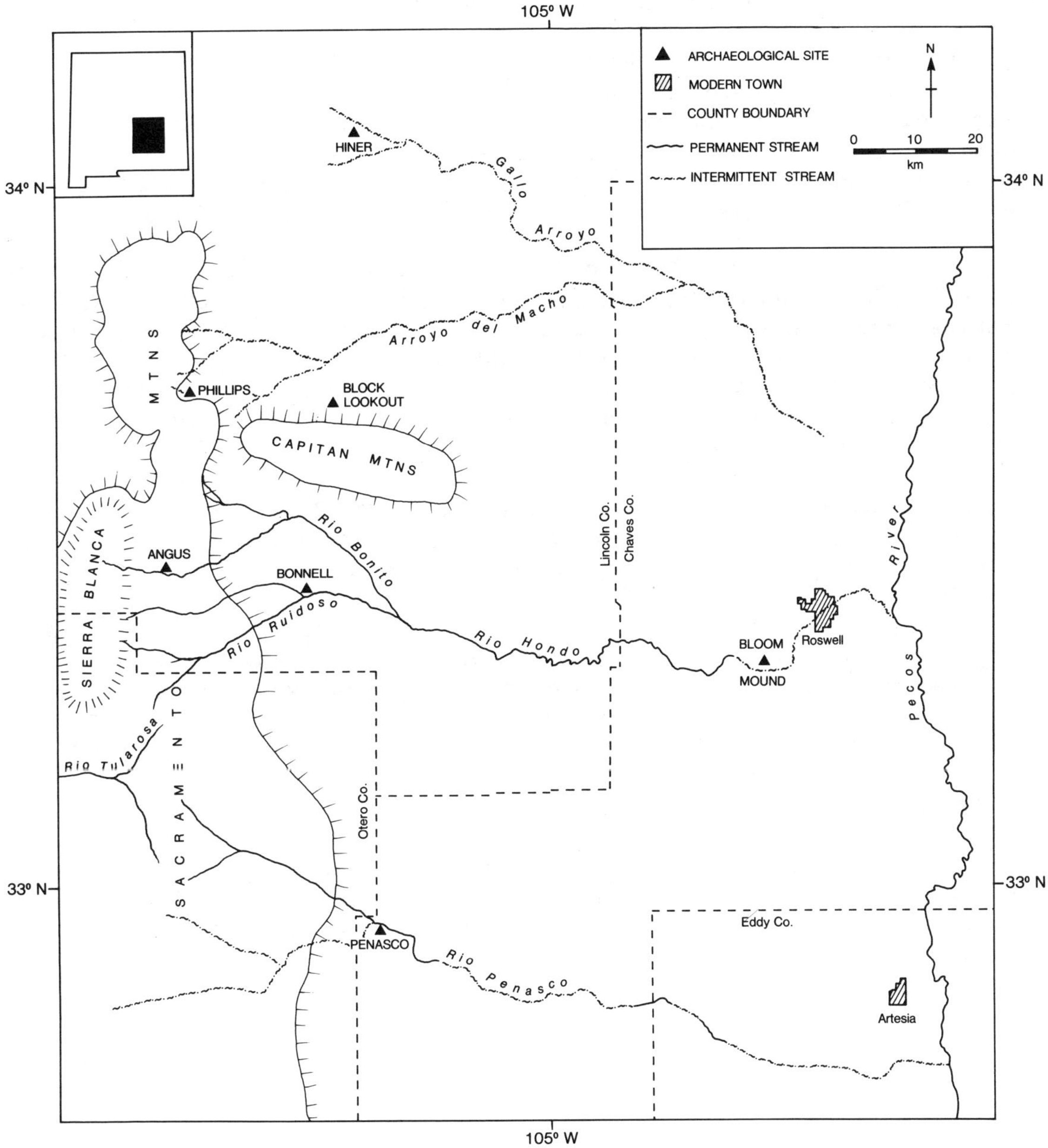

Figure 1. The Sierra Blanca region.

vegetation away from the valley margin is typical Upper Sonoran. Kelley describes the valley in summer as a "long, narrow, green oasis" (Kelley 1966:402). The site had been excavated by amateurs prior to the work of Holden and Kelley. Kelley has described four building periods. The majority of faunal remains derive from the fill of period 2 and 3 rooms. However, it is important to realize that Kelley's building periods are architectural; the date of the fill of such rooms is not necessarily related to the sequence of room construction.

The Penasco site (also described as Site 2000) is the most southerly site considered in this analysis. It is situated on a terrace of the Rio Penasco whose valley also forms something of an "oasis" in the dry Upper Sonoran vegetation. Excavations at the site exposed a complete pithouse, a partial pithouse, and two isolated floors. The site dates to the latter half of the Glencoe Phase.

To the north of the Glencoe Phase sites, occupations can be placed either in the Corona or Lincoln phases. Only one site in this study contains Corona Phase faunal material. The Phillips site is located on both sides of Carrizo Creek, in grassland close to the piñon-juniper zone. Of a total of 49 house units located, a single Corona Phase room was excavated. Two rooms and a pit of early Lincoln Phase and 14 rooms of late Lincoln Phase were excavated.

The Block Lookout site is situated on a waterless hill to the north of Capitan Mountain. Seven adobe-walled rooms were investigated, as well as a probable kiva. The site dates to the Lincoln Phase.

The Hiner site is situated well to the north of other sites in the study area, but still belongs to the Lincoln Phase. Six rooms were excavated and subfloor tests into cultural material were made.

Bloom Mound lies outside the Sierra Blanca region, in the lower Hondo Valley about 16 km above the junction of the Hondo and Pecos. Kelley suggests that the inhabitants of the site undertook extensive trading (1966:573-593). Amateur archaeologists worked at the site for a number of years; only minor excavations were undertaken by Texas Technological College. The site is assigned to the Lincoln Phase, although it is an "outlier" in terms of the normal distribution of such sites.

2
FAUNAL ANALYSIS

Methodology

Dealing with "Old" Assemblages

Given the concern with sample quality in zooarchaeology, one may ask whether analysis of bones collected in the 1950s is justified. There are certainly problems with the sample. Excavations were primarily directed towards the establishment of a regional chronology and phase definition. The majority of bones are from room fill, and little attention seems to have been given to excavation of other deposits. On the other hand, deposits were screened through a one-quarter inch (6 mm) mesh, and it appears that the excavators were conservative in keeping scraps of bone which might well have been discarded by many excavators at that time. The relatively high proportion of "unidentifiable" bone is similar, in my experience, to sites where careful screening has been undertaken. The lack of finer screening has resulted in certain biases: many rodents are represented primarily by the larger bones, and some of the smallest mammals (e.g., *Peromyscus*, *Microtus*, *Thomomys*) are represented almost exclusively by mandibles and crania. The larger rodents and the lagomorphs lack most of the phalanges and many vertebrae. Nevertheless, many modern excavators still use only six millimeter mesh, and there is no reason to believe that the screeners of the 1950s were any less competent than those of today.

Recent excavations at the Block Lookout site, renamed the Smokey Bear site (LA2112), have recovered faunal remains in essentially the same proportions of species as recovered by Holden and Kelley (Heller 1976). The results of the more recent analysis show that the excavation techniques employed in the 1950s produced results which are comparable to those resulting from more modern methods.

Probably the most important concern is the lack of contextual information available for the samples. As knowledge of site formation processes has increased, it has become apparent that faunal remains are not randomly distributed in deposits, and that patterned distribution is not necessarily the result of patterned human behavior but also the result of patterned refuse disposal and a variety of taphonomic processes. Objects recovered from pithouses or surface rooms in the Southwest may derive from a variety of sources, including use-related deposition, primary garbage deposition, secondary deposition, or (especially in the case of animal remains) intrusions. Although the lack of detailed contextual information reduces the value of the assemblages, it need not preclude analysis, although one must obviously be fairly cautious in making any conclusions.

As well as considering problems of methodology, one must also consider the value of studying assemblages collected decades ago, especially in an area so subject to the depredations of pothunters and poorly supervised amateurs. Archaeological resources are not limitless, and we cannot solve our lack of data by excavating increasingly rare pristine sites with methods which will seem primitive to the next generation of zooarchaeologists. Storage rooms of archaeological institutions of North America are replete with faunal material awaiting basic description and analysis. We need to develop methods which allow us to maximize the information retrievable from extant assemblages, and let these analyses assist in posing questions to be answered by judicious excavations in the future. In order to do this, one must attempt to develop methodological approaches which take into account the nature of previous excavations and recovery procedures. In an attempt to produce such a methodology, this analysis has been conducted under the following guidelines, which, with modifications, could be applied to the analysis of many assemblages collected in past decades:

1. One should expect bones or bone fragments below a certain size range to have been missed by excavators. Consequently, absence of such bones should be interpreted with caution.

2. Detailed comparisons between species of approximately the same size are valid, but comparisons between species of different sizes should make allowances for biases resulting from recovery procedures.

3. Comparisons between assemblages are only valid if recovery methods were similar.

4. The extent to which an assemblage from a site can be subdivided by the zooarchaeologist must take into account the quality of provenience, the type of excavation methods employed, and the adequacy of the interpretation of depositional processes at the site. It is better to be a "lumper" than a "splitter" of assemblages if the criteria for "splitting" are weak.

5. The overall aim of the analysis should be to establish general patterns which are likely to transcend possible sampling errors or vagaries of excavation methods.

Identification and Recording

For each site, bones were removed from bags, labelled, and sorted into taxonomic groups. For reasons explained later, the site assemblages are treated as single units. Only mammals are considered in detail in this report, although birds, reptiles, amphibians, and invertebrates were present in the assemblages in small amounts.

Identifications were made largely on the basis of comparative material at Simon Fraser University and the University of Calgary. However, lack of certain specimens necessitated recourse to osteological keys, of which Olsen (1964) was the most frequently consulted. Lawrence's (1951) guide to post-cranial ungulate skeletons was employed, but identifications to genus or species were made on the basis of direct comparisons with modern skeletons.

Bones were assigned to a species or genus only when identification was positive. While this statement seems obvious, many zooarchaeologists are consistently negligent in informing readers as to the nature of identification criteria. For example, the only identified large ungulate in the Sierra Blanca assemblages is *Bison*. Some zooarchaeologists would assume that all large ungulate bones were from *Bison* (an assumption which is frequently made, with some validity, at *Bison* kill sites). However, *Cervus* was also present in the region prehistorically, and it is certainly invalid to assume that all large ungulates are *Bison*. Even if there were no other large ungulates apart from *Bison* in the area, I would argue that it is still incorrect to make such an assumption, because it results in confusing data presentation. It is surely better to list as "identified" only that which is identified positively. Other material may be listed as, for example, "large ungulate." The analyst and other researchers may, if they wish, assume that "large ungulate" equals *Bison*; however, to make the assumption *prior* to presentation of raw data is unjustified.

The result of this policy is that most identifications to a species or genus have been made on cranial or mandibular fragments or on long bones with at least one articular surface. In fact, most species identifications have been made because a particular genus contains only one species. Thus *Ondatra zibethicus* is reported rather than *Ondatra*, and *Antilocapra americana* rather than *Antilocapra*. Generally, the genus level has been used for identifications when two similar species are known to have been present in the Sierra Blanca region. If species or genus could not be identified, family level was also used. This has been done for the long bones of *Spermophilus* and *Cynomys* which were collectively assigned to the category "large sciurid" because the lack of good comparative material frequently prevented accurate separation, especially of fragmentary and/or immature specimens. Beyond the family level, most bones were assigned to "small mammal" (smaller than *Lepus californicus*), "medium mammal" (deer size or smaller) and "large mammal" (larger than deer). However, a few special categories were used. "Small rodent" was used for bones which could not be identified positively because of poor comparative material. "Fox" is used for long bones which are obviously small Canidae, but cannot be assigned positively to either *Urocyon* or *Vulpes*. "Medium ungulate" is used for the many bones which are either from deer, antelope, or sheep but which cannot be assigned accurately.

"Large ungulate" is used for bones which are either from *Bison* or *Cervus*.

Once identifications were made, the following information was recorded for each specimen, when applicable: taxon, element, proportion of element present (in tenths), side, breakage unit (see below), type of break (see below), state of fusion, burning, presence of cutmarks, carnivore/rodent modification, and standard measurements following the system of von den Driesch (1976). Most of these data types are commonly used and require no further explanation. The term "breakage unit" is a substitute for Brumley's (1973) "butchery unit," and avoids the connotation that all bone breaks are the result of butchering activity. The breakage unit is a simple method for describing which part of a bone is present. Breakage units were defined for major bone types, and definitions are presented in Table 1. "Type of break" was an attempt to quantify different types of fracture in the assemblages. The categories used are not as well defined as I would now like to use, but are of some utility. Breakage types are presented in Table 2.

TABLE 1
BREAKAGE UNITS, CODE NUMBERS, AND NDP VALUES

Bone Type	Code	Description	NDP
Cranial	1	Whole	2
	2	Right or left maxilla	1
	3	Maxilla fragment	1
	4	Other cranial fragment	
Antler/	1	Whole	1
Horn core	2	Fragment attached to cranium	1
	3	Other fragment	
Mandible	1	Whole	1
	2	Posterior to m3	
	3	Anterior to p2	
	4	Complete tooth row	1
	5	Fragment of tooth row	1
	6	2 plus 5	1
	7	3 plus 5	1
	8	Ramus fragment	
Hyoid	1	Whole	
	2	Fragment	
Vertebrae	1	Whole	1
	2	Fragment	
	3	Centrum	1
	4	Medio-lateral split centrum	1
	5	Unfused epiphysis	
	6	Fetal vertebra fragment	

TABLE 1 (continued)

Bone Type	Code	Description	NDP
Rib	1	Whole	2
	2	Proximal	1
	3	Distal	1
	4	Shaft fragment	
	5	Ossified costal cartilage	
Sternum	1	Whole	
	2	Fragment	
Scapula	1	Whole	1
	2	Fragment including glenoid	1
	3	Blade fragment	
Pelvis	1	Whole left or right	1
	2	Fragment with ilium, pubis, acetabulum, ischium	1
	3	Ilium fragment	
	4	Acetabulum	1
	5	Ilium plus acetabulum	1
	6	Pubis and/or ischium	
	7	Pubis/ischium plus acetabulum	1
	8	Other fragment	
Long bones	1	Whole	2
	2	Proximal plus half shaft	1
	3	Proximal plus less than half shaft	1
	4	Proximal unfused epiphysis without diaphysis	1
	5	Distal plus half shaft	1
	6	Distal plus less than half shaft	1
	7	Distal unfused epiphysis without diaphysis	1
	8	Shaft fragment	
Carpal, tarsal, sesamoid	1	Whole	1
	2	Fragment	
1st, 2nd phal.	1	Whole	2
	2	Proximal	1
	3	Proximal unfused epiphysis	1
	4	Distal	1
	5	Shaft fragment	
3rd phal.	1	Whole	1
	2	Proximal	1
	3	Distal	
Axial, unident.	8	Fragment	

TABLE 2
DEFINITIONS OF BREAKAGE TYPES

Breakage Type	Description
Intact	No breakage, or only minor surface erosion or abrasion.
Excavator	When possible, bones broken during excavation were glued together. However, some bones exhibited breaks made during excavation but corresponding fragments could not be found.
Spiral	Spiral fracture with smooth break surfaces.
Transverse	Fracture perpendicular to long axis of bone. Equals "horizontal tension failure" (Johnson 1983:60).
Splintered	Irregular break, usually with jagged edges formed by longitudinal and perpendicular fractures. If carnivore activity resulted in splintering, this was noted separately.

The Assemblages

For each site, all bones have been considered as a single assemblage. At a number of sites--Bloom Mound, Block Lookout, Hiner, and Penasco--the sample is too small for further subdivision. At Phillips and Bonnell a substantial number of rooms were excavated and bones can be located fairly confidently within particular structures. In spite of this, there are good reasons for not conducting intra-site analyses based upon subdivided assemblages. First, as Kelley's study of the pottery at Bonnell demonstrates, the fill of the structures may well be secondary because pottery "fits" occur across stratigraphic boundaries (Kelley 1979:112). Faunal analysis provides further suggestion of this because a bone "fit" occurred between structures. Secondly, although there is evidence for variation in faunas from room to room at Bonnell (Kelley 1979:113), it is difficult to analyze this variation with any degree of confidence because one cannot establish sequences of filling for the various structures. Spatial variation in disposal of faunal material is predictable at archaeological sites (e.g., Halstead et al. 1978; Maltby 1982; Meadow 1978). Until one has better control of stratigraphy than is possible for the sites considered in this paper, spatial variation is interesting to document but of little analytical value. The way in which pueblo rooms or pithouses become filled is an area of research which surely demands considerable attention (Raish et al. 1984).

Post-depositional preservation of bone seems good at most sites: few bones exhibit longitudinal weathering cracks; fetal or neonatal ungulates are represented; and there is good skeletal representation for animals such as the medium-sized ungulates where sullegic factors have not intervened. The only exception to this is Bloom Mound where preservation is obviously poorer and where bones have a powdery surface and frequent weathering breaks.

Data Presentation

Raw data on each taxonomic group at each site are presented in Appendix A. The tables provide information on element and breakage unit frequency; breakage units are defined in Table 1. The tables also provide three separate quantification systems--NISP, NDP, and MNI.

NISP (number of identified specimens) is the raw count of bones identified to each taxon. This is the basic and least controversial aspect of quantification, from which other indices of abundance can be derived. The NISP method has numerous well known problems (see Grayson 1979 for a summary). In order to partially circumvent these problems, I use a method called NDP (number of diagnostic points). The NDP method defines for each anatomical element certain diagnostic points. Bone fragments which contain a diagnostic point are counted as "1" in the NDP system. A fragment which contains two diagnostic points is counted as "2." A fragment which possesses no diagnostic point is not counted, even though it may be identifiable to the species level. Definitions of NDP values are presented in Table 1. For example, a complete mammal long bone counts as "2" in the NDP system--one point for each end. A mammal proximal long bone would count as "1" NDP, and a shaft fragment would count as "0." Similar systems to NDP have been advanced by other zooarchaeologists, such as Watson (1979). The main advantage of NDP over NISP is that it avoids problems of differential fragmentation and identifiability associated with the NISP method. For example, the bones of larger mammals tend to be broken into more pieces than those of smaller mammals, and NISP will thus over-exaggerate the importance of larger animals at the expense of the smaller. The NDP method minimizes (although does not eliminate) such errors by only counting certain parts of bones rather than every fragment. As another example, most zooarchaeologists are aware that certain bones in the mammalian skeleton (such as ungulate tibiae) produce readily identifiable small fragments, whereas similar-sized fragments of other bones cannot be identified to element. NISP will tend to overemphasize the presence of the easily identified bones, whereas NDP tends to standardize counts by selecting only more easily identified areas (such as long-bone ends) for counting.

In this study I will use both NDP and NISP quantification methods, the latter being required when comparisons are made to other published assemblages. In general, it will be seen that NISP and NDP values correlate well. However, for large mammals NDP is usually less than NISP because large mammal bones are heavily fragmented. For smaller mammals one often sees that lagomorphs have a lower NDP than NISP whereas sciurids have a higher NDP than NISP. This results from differential fragmentation of the bones of the two orders.

MNI (minimum number of individuals) has been calculated using Grayson's minimum distinction method for the entire assemblage. No attempt was made to match pairs of bones, and the MNI values are based upon left/right distinctions and fused/unfused categories. I do not regard MNI as a useful quantification method at the Sierra Blanca sites, and the data are provided purely for comparative purposes. For arguments against the use of MNI see Grayson (1979).

Taxonomic Categories

In this section I discuss the taxonomic categories used in this report. Discussion of the general criteria of identification has been presented above. Details of specific identification procedures are provided below.

Amphibian

A few long bones were found at Bonnell and Penasco, presumably as a result of the riverine location. No species identification was made.

Reptile

The only recognizable reptile remains were fragments of turtle carapace, which are quite likely to have been artifacts.

Bird

Bird bones were present at all sites, generally forming less than 5% of any assemblage, except at Block Lookout where they formed 14% of the NDP total. Identification of birds was not undertaken because of poor comparative collections. At Bonnell 166 bird bones represented at least eight species including turkey and eagle. Penasco produced seven bird bones. Phillips contained 30 bird bones representing at least six species, including turkey and eagle. The 37 bird bones recovered from Block Lookout included turkey. Hiner produced one bird bone, and Bloom Mound produced two.

Mammal

Order Lagomorpha

The following lagomorph bones were identified to genus level when possible: cranial, mandible, vertebra, scapula, humerus, radius, ulna, metacarpus, pelvis, femur, tibia, tarsals, metatarsus. All other elements were included in the "small mammal" class.

The majority of lagomorph bones were identified as *Sylvilagus*. The species was not identified, but both *S. audubonii* and *S. floridanus* could be represented. Cottontails do not construct major burrows, but they do inhabit burrows of other animals, such as prairie dogs (Bailey 1931:55). Their presence on a site must therefore be treated with suspicion, although all lagomorphs were important food items for historic southwestern cultures.

Lepus is readily distinguished from *Sylvilagus* in the Southwest by its greater size. Species identification was not undertaken, although *L. americanus* is excluded by virtue of its smaller size. *L. californicus* is the common species of the modern Upper Sonoran zone and is more likely to be represented than *L. townsendii*. Jackrabbits do not dig or commonly inhabit burrows.

Order Rodentia

Family Sciuridae. Only mandibles and maxillae were identified to genus. Vertebra, scapula, humerus, radius, ulna, pelvis, femur, and tibia were identified only as "large sciurid." Other elements were included in "small rodents" or "small mammal."

The sciurids form an important component of many North American faunas. However, identification of the sciurid rodents from the six assemblages was made difficult by poor post-cranial comparative collections. Two genera were identified on the basis of mandibles and maxillae. Both *Spermophilus* and *Cynomys* are found in the Upper Sonoran habitat, and both dig and inhabit burrows. The modern *Cynomys* in the area is *C. ludovicianus* and this is probably the species represented at the sites. At least three species of *Spermophilus* occur in the area today, but *S. variegatus* is probably represented, on the basis of the size of the mandibles.

Family Geomyidae. Mandibles and maxillae of *Thomomys* were present at some sites, with occasional post-cranial elements. Most post-cranial bones were absent, almost certainly the result of screening through a 6 mm mesh. Pocket gophers inhabit extensive burrows, and are likely to be intrusive on archaeological sites.

Family Muridae. Mandibles of *Peromyscus* were occasionally recovered, but post-cranial elements were largely missed during excavations. They probably represent natural deaths.

Neotoma was also represented by mandibles and some post-cranial elements. Pack rats might well inhabit abandoned pithouses and surface rooms, but they could represent food items.

The presence of *Ondatra zibethicus* at Bonnell and Penasco is probably due to its distribution along permanent watercourses in New Mexico (Bailey 1931:208). A variety of cranial and post-cranial elements were recovered. Muskrats might well have been trapped for their fur, and are unlikely to have been indigenous inhabitants of the abandoned sites.

Microtus is represented by occasional mandibles.

Family *Erethizontidae*. A single mandible from Bonnell was identified as porcupine (*Erethizon dorsatum*). It is not possible to say whether the specimen represents the remains of food, although they are quite edible.

Order Carnivora

Family *Canidae*. Three genera of canids are found in the Sierra Blanca region today--*Canis*, *Urocyon*, and *Vulpes*. *Canis* is distinguished from the others by its greater size. *Urocyon* and *Vulpes* are most easily distinguished on the basis of cranial characters.

For most specimens of *Canis* it was difficult to distinguish between dog (*C. familiaris*) and coyote (*C. latrans*). However, no elements were of sufficient size to warrant classification as wolf (*C. lupus*). Both coyote and dog are likely to be found at sites in the area. A mandible and maxilla from Bonnell were clearly dog, on the basis of tooth crowding and tooth size. The majority of bones were post-cranial, and fit within size ranges for either species.

Foxes were identified at Bonnell and Phillips. A complete scapula at Phillips has been identified as *Vulpes velox* (now considered to encompass specimens formerly classified as both *V. velox* and *V. macrotis*, according to Hall 1981). At Bonnell a mandible, maxilla, and cranial vault were positively identified as *Urocyon cinereoargenteus*, the grey fox. A number of post-cranial elements were also recovered, but have been classified simply as "fox," even though they probably belong to *Urocyon*.

Family *Ursidae*. The root of a very large carnivore canine at Bonnell fits best with a bear canine. Species determination was not possible.

Family *Mustelidae*. An almost complete mandible of *Mustela frenata* was recovered from Bonnell. The long-tailed weasel was probably a post-occupational inhabitant of the site.

Taxidea taxus, the badger, was represented by a pair of innominates from Phillips. It, too, may have been a post-occupation inhabitant.

The most common mustelid was the striped skunk, *Mephitis mephitis*, represented by cranial and post-cranial elements at Bonnell and Penasco.

Family Felidae. *Felis concolor*, the cougar, was recovered from Bonnell and Phillips. Only foot bones were found. These animals have been severely reduced throughout most of their range by modern controls, and it is likely that they ranged more widely in the past. Bailey (1931:285) indicates that they ranged away from the mountains when game was abundant, and they were probably the major large predator (apart from humans) in the Sierra Blanca. The presence of foot bones may show that they were hunted for their skin.

Lynx rufus is represented at all sites except Hiner and Bloom Mound. Definite speciation is only possible on a mandible from Bonnell, but as *Lynx canadensis* is confined to more northerly latitudes, *L. rufus*, the bobcat, is presumably responsible for all the *Lynx* bones.

Order Artiodactyla

Family Cervidae. Both mule deer (*Odocoileus hemionus*) and white-tailed deer (*O. virginianus*) are present in the Sierra Blanca region today. *Odocoileus* is present at all sites, although only antler is present at Bloom Mound. Speciation was not possible as cranial and antler specimens were fragmentary.

Deer was only identified when it could be distinguished from pronghorn or sheep. Such distinctions were made on skull, mandible, scapula, pelvis, and all leg bones. No attempt was made to identify vertebrae, ribs, and sternum to genus. Immature deer bones are difficult to distinguish from those of similar-sized ungulates, and distinctions were not always possible on unfused bones or fetal specimens. Most identified deer and pronghorn bones are from skeletally mature individuals.

Family Antilocapridae. As only one species of this family occurs, *Antilocapra americana* can be identified with confidence once the family or genus is recorded. Identification methods for antelope were the same as for deer.

Pronghorns occurred widely in open areas of New Mexico prior to the twentieth century. Although their range overlaps that of the deer, diets are different. Pronghorns consume grass and forbs (Bailey 1931:26; Davis 1960:224); deer are primarily browsers. Antelope are particularly well adapted to xeric conditions, and require less water than deer. Pronghorns have been identified in all assemblages.

Family Bovidae. The American bison (*Bison bison*) and the bighorn sheep (*Ovis canadensis*) were both present in eastern New Mexico, but only bison is present at sites included in this study. I was not able to confirm Kooyman's (n.d.) identification of a few specimens of bighorn sheep at Bonnell. Bison was only identified when it could be positively separated from elk (*Cervus elaphus*). Most fragments which have been identified as "large ungulate" are very likely from bison.

Origin of the Faunas

A major interpretive problem faced by many zooarchaeologists is the origin of faunal remains found in association with artifacts and structures, and a considerable literature is devoted to this topic (Gifford 1981). This problem is critical in the case of animals which form an important quantitative component of an assemblage, but which could owe their origin on the site to agencies other than human exploitation. The Sierra Blanca assemblages pose problems of this type.

Attempts to solve such problems have been proposed by various zooarchaeologists. Thomas (1971) suggested that Shotwell's (1955) index of skeletal completeness be used. Such a method cannot be employed on assemblages where recovery methods introduce bias, and major criticisms of the method have been made on other grounds (Grayson 1978). Most taphonomic studies by archaeologists and paleontologists have tended to stress mammals in the upper size ranges, and have concentrated upon the presence of cut marks (e.g., Binford 1981; Bunn 1981), element frequency (e.g., Binford 1981; Brain 1981), and evidence for carnivore activity (e.g., Binford 1981; Brain 1981; Haynes 1982). At the Sierra Blanca sites there is very little doubt that the larger mammals are the result of human activity, because the bones of deer, antelope, and bison show little carnivore damage, exhibit cut marks, demonstrate very little differential element loss, and have been recovered from room fill.

Less attention has been paid to identifying the origin of smaller components of faunal assemblages (Korth 1979:236). This is probably because the number of taphonomic routes from living populations to paleontological or archaeological sites is greater for small animals. Typical North American rodents are preyed upon by a wider range of animals than typical North American artiodactyls, which suffer major predation from top carnivores. Rodents are also more likely to inhabit and die within archaeological sites as a result of fossorial behavior. Rodent bones are more prone to fluvial transportation. Finally, a scatological origin for identifiable rodent faunas is much more likely than for the larger mammals. For many archaeological sites the possible origin for the bones of large mammals can often be ascribed to either large carnivores or human predation. (This is not to discount a variety of other mechanisms which have been documented; I am simply stating that these are two very common alternatives.) However, the presence of small mammals on archaeological sites often requires the testing of multiple origins, many of which do not leave distinct patterns of breakage or other modification on the bone. Excluding a fluvial origin for the Sierra Blanca small mammals, three general hypotheses can be proposed to account for their origin:

1. They are the product of human procurement, the bones representing the discarded remains of animals procured by deliberate hunting or trapping. Such animals may be procured for food or for raw material.

2. They represent animals which lived and died on the site either during or after the human occupation. The animals were not consumed by predators or scavengers.

3. They are the remnants of animals either killed by non-human predators or utilized by scavengers. The predators may have been living on the site or visiting the site to hunt. The bones may have never entered the digestive tract (meal remnants), may have entered the tract and been regurgitated (e.g., as owl pellets), or may have been passed through the tract (i.e., deposited as fecal material). These processes have been reviewed by Korth (1979).

Although all small mammals at the Sierra Blanca sites require analysis to derive a taphonomic history, relatively few taxa will be subjected to detailed study. Most taxa are represented by so few bones that it is impossible to discuss their origin on the site. For example, the *Microtus* mandibles from Bonnell might be the result of any of the processes outlined in the three hypotheses above, but no definite statement about their origin can be made. Three groups of animals have been selected for detailed consideration--the large sciurids (*Spermophilus* and *Cynomys*), *Sylvilagus*, and *Lepus*. These have been selected because they are numerous in some assemblages. In order to investigate the three hypotheses presented previously, the habits of the various taxa can be considered initially, as these may provide certain "limiting factors" in their taphonomic history.

Cynomys colonies were frequent west of the Pecos in the Upper Sonoran zone (Bailey 1931:123). Colonies were extensive, covering hundreds of acres in some cases. Major predators included badgers, coyotes, eagles, and hawks. There is no reason to suppose that prairie dog "towns" could not be located on an abandoned archaeological site. However, prairie dogs would certainly be palatable, and could constitute a source of meat for humans. *Spermophilus* was identified only at Bonnell. It also constructs burrows, is hunted by predators similar to those of *Cynomys*, and could serve as a human food source.

Sylvilagus, regardless of species, does not construct burrows, but will occupy the burrows of other animals (Bailey 1931; Davis 1960). Prairie dog burrows are frequently occupied, although a wide range of other shelters may be used. Major predators include coyotes, foxes, eagles, owls, and snakes. *Sylvilagus* was widely hunted in the Southwest, and formed an important component of ritual activity (Tyler 1964).

Lepus does not excavate burrows and rarely occupies them. Major predators are similar to Sylvilagus. Jackrabbits were important in diet and myth of the Southwest villages.

From the above accounts it can be seen that many mechanisms could result in the deposition of small mammal bones on archaeological sites. As there is no reason to exclude either cultural or natural origins for the small mammals found at the Sierra Blanca sites, a methodology is required to distinguish between natural and cultural bones. The three hypotheses presented above can be investigated by considering what a faunal assemblage would look like if produced predominantly by one of the three major proposed mechanisms.

Natural deaths of animals on sites, particularly in burrows, should produce complete skeletons with largely intact bones if the animals remain undisturbed. However, subsequent burrowing is likely to produce scattered, disarticulated skeletons, although still with predominantly complete bones. Broken bones should exhibit fractures typical of dessicated or leached specimens, rather than green bone fractures.

Bones resulting from animal predation (or bones from scavenged carcasses) will exhibit patterns of damage typical of the species consuming the prey. Such patterns are likely to be very variable. For example, different owls produce different breakage patterns (Dodson and Wexlar 1979) and differential digestive erosion of bones (Lowe 1980).

The size relationship between consumer and consumed will also have an effect (compare, for example, damage to medium and large ungulate bones as a result of wolf killing described by Binford 1981 and Haynes 1982). Furthermore, the activity of the consumer and, no doubt, its hunger level will also play a role. Teeth marks should be present if the predator or scavenger is fairly small (e.g., fox eating rabbit) but may be absent if the predator is very large (e.g., coyote eating mouse). Breakage patterns may range from essentially complete elements in owl pellets (Dodson and Wexlar 1979) to macerated fragments contained in coyote scats (Korth 1979). One should expect to find green bone fractures resulting from certain predators.

Based upon coprolite evidence (Callen 1967, 1969:242), it would appear that humans do not often ingest large bone fragments from animals the size of a prairie dog or rabbit. Cultural variation in the preparation of small mammals is likely, and one might expect to find bones left relatively complete, heavily macerated, or at almost any stage in between. For example, one could compare the human treatment of dassies in Africa (Brain 1981) with treatment of monkeys and other small/medium mammals by the Aché of South America (Jones 1983). Tyler's (1964) account of rabbits in Pueblo culture includes descriptions of rabbits roasted whole and rabbit bones ground to a powder. Given our current knowledge about human consumption of small mammals, there is no set of criteria which can be applied, except the presence of cut marks or patterned burning (Vigne and Marinval-Vigne 1983), which would certainly indicate some human use of the animal. Certainly, one can predict the presence of green bone fractures resulting from certain types of human butchery. However, it would appear to be impossible to distinguish many of these from similar breaks made by predators and scavengers.

All of the above criteria are based upon the state of the bones. It is possible that one could use contextual information to study the origin of small animal bones, particularly in such artificial deposits as filled rooms (Raish et al. 1984). Unfortunately, good contextual data for the Sierra Blanca sites are lacking and it is impossible to assess the extent to which bones derive from refuse dumping, rodent burrowing, or carnivore occupation. It would seem, therefore, that positive determination of the origin of the small mammal faunas at the Sierra Blanca sites will not be possible. Nevertheless, some suggestions can be made.

A scatological origin for the bones of the large sciurids and lagomorphs seems unlikely. Major mammalian predators of these animals, such as bobcat or coyote, will crush bones into small fragments, to be ingested and subsequently deposited in scats. I have observed *Lepus* in wolf and coyote scats, and the bone is highly comminuted. The same can be observed for other canids (Andrews and Evans 1983; Korth 1979:247-248). Smaller carnivores, such as weasels or skunks, also break bone into small pieces (Andrews and Evans 1983). While one cannot rule out the possibility that the assemblages were accumulated by very large birds, such as the Great Horned Owl, this seems unlikely, and one would have to propose that such birds roosted frequently on the site.

If natural predators are rejected as the likely agency of accumulation for the majority of large sciurids and lagomorphs, then remaining hypotheses are that the animals died on the site or were consumed by humans. As far as lagomorphs are concerned, on-site death is unlikely. Examination of the relevant breakage unit tables for *Lepus* and *Sylvilagus* in Appendix A shows that complete bones are rare, except for the smallest bones for which only whole specimens are likely to have been recovered by the excavation procedures. I conclude that the majority of lagomorph bones owe their origin on the sites to human predation, although one cannot discount the possiblity that a variety of predators and natural deaths may have contributed a small portion of the assemblages. Given our knowledge of Southwestern groups at the time of European contact, the presence of lagomorphs as food items is expected.

However, large sciurids still pose a problem. Very high percentages of large sciurid long bones are complete, in contrast to those of the lagomorphs. Table 3 presents the data from the two largest assemblages--Bonnell and Phillips.

Complete bones are consistent with the hypothesis that the bones are of natural, rather than cultural, origin; complete bones are very unlikely to be the result of natural predation by mammalian carnivores.

Furthermore, examination of the types of break exhibited by large sciurid bones also provides further evidence for believing natural on-site death to be a major factor in the accumulation of these specimens. If one considers the three major long bones--humerus, femur, and tibia--there are differences in the frequency of the types of break for *Sylvilagus* and the large sciurids.

TABLE 3
COMPARISON OF LONG-BONE BREAKAGE FOR *SYLVILAGUS* AND LARGE SCIURIDS FROM BONNELL AND PHILLIPS

	Bonnell		Phillips	
	Whole	Proximal or Distal End	Whole	Proximal or Distal End
Sylvilagus				
Humerus	1	75	0	5
Radius	10	20	2	2
Ulna	5	30	1	4
Femur	2	148	2	30
Tibia	1	115	1	33
Total	19	388	6	74
Percentage	4.7	95.3	7.5	92.5
Large sciurid				
Humerus	29	32	9	8
Radius	7	4	1	2
Ulna	8	12	2	1
Femur	23	42	10	7
Tibia	21	41	3	6
Total	88	131	25	24
Percentage	40.2	59.8	51.0	49.0

As can be seen from Table 4, 51% of the breaks in *Sylvilagus* were classified as spiral fractures, in contrast to only 20% in the large sciurids. Furthermore, 27% of the broken large sciurid bones are transverse snaps, made when the bone was dry, as opposed to only 13% of these same elements in *Sylvilagus*. While one cannot rule out the possibility that the large sciurids, notably *Cynomys*, formed a component of the diet of Sierra Blanca people, available data suggest that many of the bones were probably not the result of human hunting, as long as we assume that complete bones are an unlikely product of that process. I shall therefore exclude the large sciurids as definite dietary items.

To conclude, I am prepared to accept that the bones of *Odocoileus*, *Antilocapra*, and *Bison* are definitely the result of human hunting and subsequent transportation and disposal. *Lepus* and *Sylvilagus* are probably also the result of these processes. It is likely that *Ursus*, *Felis*, *Lynx*, and *Canis* are also associated with human activity, but samples are too small to be analyzed in detail. Even though these taxa are potentially edible, their contribution (if any) to the diet of the site's inhabitants is apparently minimal. I regard the status of all other identified mammalian taxa as uncertain. However, with the exception of the large sciurids, these taxa form such a small proportion of the excavated assemblages that they can be ignored in considerations of major subsistence patterns. In fact, it is likely that most are post-depositional inhabitants of the abandoned villages. As stated above, I consider the large sciurids are probable intrusive elements in the assemblages in spite of their high frequencies at certain sites.

TABLE 4
BREAKAGE PATTERNS ON HUMERUS, FEMUR, AND TIBIA OF LARGE SCIURIDS AND *SYLVILAGUS*, BONNELL SITE

	Breakage Type					
	Spiral	%	Splintered	%	Transverse	%
Sylvilagus	218	51.1	154	36.1	55	12.9
Large sciurid	28	20.1	74	53.2	37	26.6

The Lagomorph Assemblage

Element Frequency

Because collection and identification procedures have obviously affected element frequency, only skull, mandible, scapula, pelvis, and major long bones are considered for *Sylvilagus* and *Lepus*. Element frequency data are presented in Tables 5 and 6.

For *Sylvilagus*, elements of the hindlimb outnumber those of the forelimb. Although rabbit forelimbs are poor sources of meat compared to hindlimbs, the greater frequency of hindlimb elements need not necessarily indicate human selectivity for the hindlimb; one should also consider that hindlimb elements in lagomorphs are larger than forelimb elements and that their chances of being recovered are therefore higher. It is worth noting that there is no significant difference in the frequency of *Lepus* fore- and hindlimbs. *Lepus* bones are larger than those of *Sylvilagus*, and it may be that the smaller *Sylvilagus* bones were subject to greater bias during collection.

TABLE 5
ELEMENT FREQUENCY DATA (NDP) FOR SYLVILAGUS

	Bonnell	Penasco	Phillips	Block	Hiner	Bloom
Cranial	46	1	8	1		
Mandible	154	4	22	2		
Scapula	61	3	9			
Hum. Prox.	39	1	4		2	
Hum. Dist.	38		1	1	1	
Rad. Prox.	23	1	3	1		
Rad. Dist.	17	2	3	1		
Uln. Prox.	32	3	4			
Uln. Dist.	8		2			
Mc. Prox.	6			1		
Mc. Dist.	6			1		
Pelvis	154	14	24	2		2
Fem. Prox.	81	4	20	2	4	1
Fem. Dist.	71	2	14	3	3	
Tib. Prox.	82	4	30	8	1	1
Tib. Dist.	35	2	5	1	1	2
Mt. Prox.	51	2	1	1		
Mt. Dist.	44	2	1	1		

TABLE 6
ELEMENT FREQUENCY DATA (NDP) FOR LEPUS

	Bonnell	Penasco	Phillips	Block	Hiner	Bloom
Cranial	9					
Mandible	28	3	3			1
Scapula	19	5	3			
Hum. Prox.	8	4	3	1	1	
Hum. Dist.	15	6	2	1		
Rad. Prox.	16	1	5		2	
Rad. Dist.	10	1	1			
Uln. Prox.	15	2	5	2	1	
Uln. Dist.	1					
Mc. Prox.	2		1			
Mc. Dist.	2		1			
Pelvis	21	7	3	1		
Fem. Prox.	8	3	1	1		
Fem. Dist.	16	9	4	1		
Tib. Prox.	15	2	3			
Tib. Dist.	7	2	5			1
Mt. Prox.	12	3	5			
Mt. Dist.	8	1	4			

Bone Modification

There was no evidence for cut marks on any lagomorph bones. However, large numbers of bones were broken when green (see Table 4), and it is possible that lagomorph long bones were broken open for their rather small marrow content.

Bone Fusion

Fusion data for *Sylvilagus* and *Lepus* are presented in Tables 7 and 8. Relatively little is known about fusion of rabbit bones. However, a number of studies (Hale 1949; Thomson and Mortenson 1946) demonstrate that the proximal humerus and proximal tibia fuse before the animal is one year old. As these are late fusing bones in mammals, one can presume that all long-bone fusion will take place prior to this time. (I have examined one skeleton of *Lepus americanus* in which the proximal tibia and proximal humerus were unfused, and found that all other limb elements except the proximal ulna were fused, although the femur still retained fusion lines.) Thus, the frequency of unfused proximal tibiae and humeri should provide the percentage of rabbits of less than one year in an assemblage, all other factors being equal. Because unfused bones are more likely to be destroyed or lost in excavation, one cannot place too much emphasis on such estimates, although they do provide some minimum figures for the use of immature rabbits. At Bonnell, figures for the humerus and tibia show that between 38% and 48% of *Sylvilagus* were killed within their first year, and figures for the tibia at Phillips give a value of 33%. For *Lepus* at Bonnell the figures are about 25% killed within the first year. Such percentages show no marked selection for either mature or immature animals.

The Medium Ungulate Assemblage

Element Frequency

Because of difficulties in separating *Odocoileus* and *Antilocapra*, especially with immature fragmentary specimens, all medium ungulate bones are considered together for the purposes of this analysis (Table 9). Figure 2 compares the frequency of elements in medium ungulate assemblages from Bonnell and Phillips with the element frequency which would be expected in a "natural" assemblage derived from complete animal carcasses. Comparing the archaeological distribution with the "natural" distribution, there are some obvious differences. Most notably, rib frequency is reduced in the archaeological sites, generally resulting in an overrepresentation of other elements, when compared to the expected representation in a "natural" unmodified assemblage. Of the two assemblages, Phillips is more similar to a "natural" element frequency than Bonnell. This is mainly because the relative frequency of ribs and vertebrae is higher at Phillips.

TABLE 7
SYLVILAGUS fusion

U=unfused; F=fused

	Bonnell		Penasco		Phillips		Block		Hiner		Bloom	
	U	F	U	F	U	F	U	F	U	F	U	F
Scapula		61		3		9						
Hum. Prox.	15	24		1		4			1	1		
Hum. Dist.		38				1		1		1		
Rad. Prox.	1	22		1		4		1				
Rad. Dist.	4	14	1	1		4		1				
Uln. Prox.	6	26		3		4						
Uln. Dist.	3	5				2						
Mc. Dist.		6						1				
Fem. Prox.	26	54		4	6	14		2		4		1
Fem. Dist.	27	44	1	1	2	11	1	2		3		
Tib. Prox.	39	43		4	10	20	4	4	1			1
Tib. Dist.	10	25	1	1	1	3		1		1	1	1
Mt. Dist.	9	35		2		1		1				

TABLE 8
LEPUS FUSION

U=unfused; F=fused

	Bonnell		Penasco		Phillips		Block		Hiner		Bloom	
	U	F	U	F	U	F	U	F	U	F	U	F
Scapula		19		5		3						
Hum. Prox.	2	6		4		3		1		1		
Hum. Dist.		15	1	5		2		1				
Rad. Prox.	2	14		1		5				1		
Rad. Dist.	1	9		1		1						
Uln. Prox.	1	15		2		5		2	1	1		
Uln. Dist.												
Mc. Dist.		2				1						
Fem. Prox.	2	6	1	2		1		1				
Fem. Dist.	2	15		7	2	2		1				
Tib. Prox.	4	10		2		3						
Tib. Dist.	1	6	2		1	5						1
Mt. Dist.		8		1		4						

TABLE 9
NDP VALUES FOR ALL MEDIUM UNGULATE BONES

	Bonnell	Penasco	Phillips	Block	Hiner	Bloom
Cranial	19	2	14	5		
Mandible	15	3	17	3		
Cervical	11	2	32	2	1	
Thoracic	11	4	35	10	5	
Lumbar	7		34	5	1	
Sacrum			9	1		
Rib Prox.	15	1	67	8	3	
Rib Dist.	33	2	38	6		
Scapula	13	2	25	4	3	
Hum. Prox.	8	3	18	7	1	
Hum. Dist.	16	1	30	8		
Rad. Prox.	7	5	21	4	4	
Rad. Dist.	9		15	3	2	
Uln. Prox.	9		14	2		
Uln. Dist.	2		1			
Carpal	9		10	3	4	
Mc. Prox.	12	1	10	2	1	
Mc. Dist.	7	2	14	3	2	1
Pelvis	8	1	8	4	1	
Fem. Prox.	7	3	30	3	2	
Fem. Dist.	12	7	27	2	1	
Tib. Prox.	20	4	38	3	1	
Tib. Dist.	8	3	18	5	2	
Tarsal	23	7	46	2	4	1
Mt. Prox.	9	1	13	2	1	
Mt. Dist.	9		11	2	5	
1 Phal.	51	10	131	11	13	
2 Phal.	39	12	79	6	14	
3 Phal.	11	6	26	4	4	
Total	400	82	831	120	75	2

The interpretation of element frequency in any archaeological assemblage is ultimately a question of assessing the interplay of numerous factors. In spite of a wealth of evidence concerning modern assemblages (see, for example, Binford 1978, 1981; Brain 1981), relatively little use has been made of complete assemblage analysis in the interpretation of past events. Binford's analysis of the Olduvai assemblages depends to some extent upon evaluating the degree of destruction suffered by the assemblages as a result of carnivore activity (Binford 1981:256-262). Analysis of Olduvai assemblage composition (Binford 1981:262-278) is primarily concerned with evaluating whether or not assemblages were the result of various carnivore activities. In fact, Binford offers very little guidance concerning the interpretation of assemblages which are definitely accumulated by Recent humans, the very types of assemblage with which

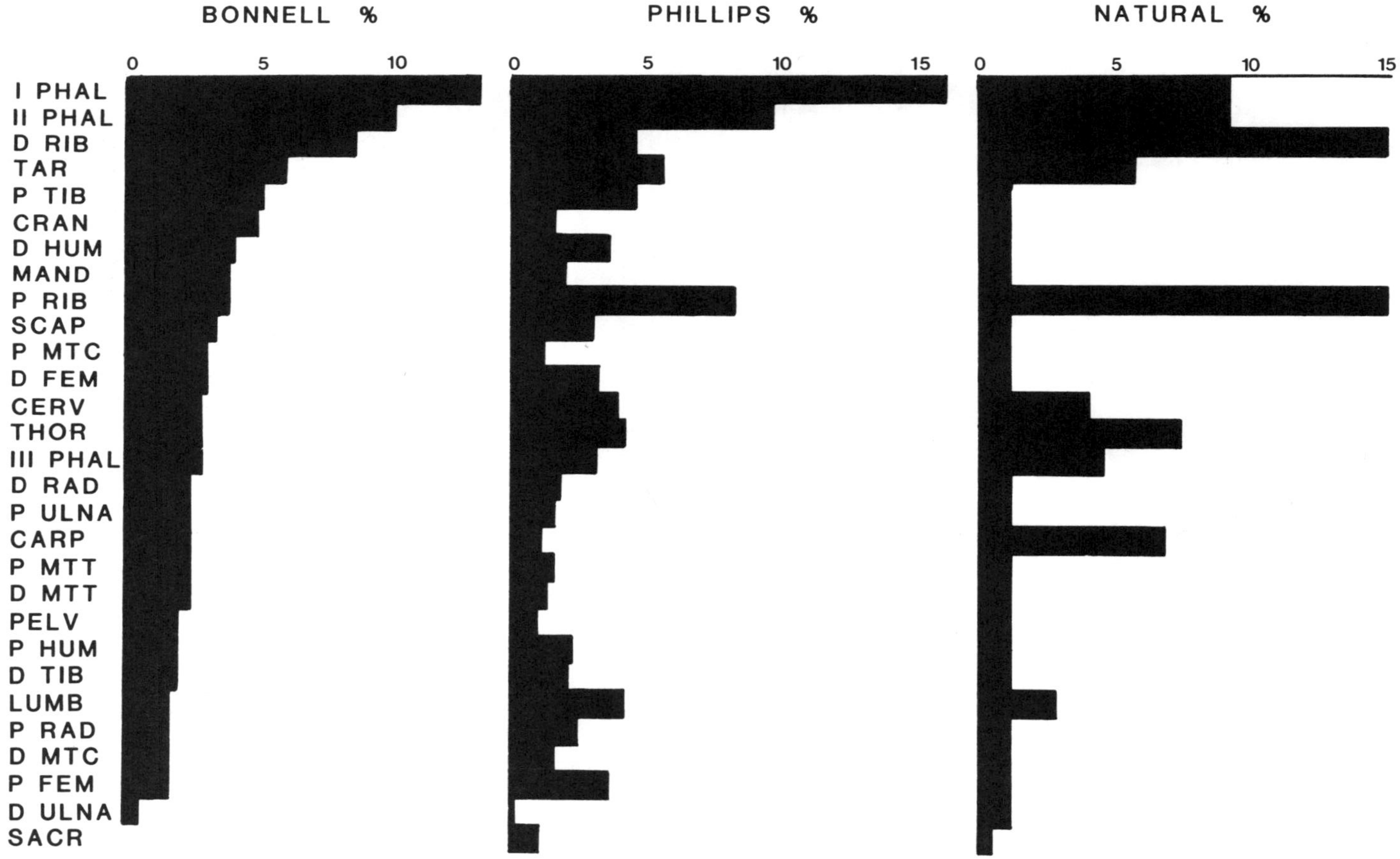

Figure 2. Deer, antelope, and medium ungulate element frequency at Bonnell and Phillips, compared with the natural element frequency. Note that frequency is expressed as a percentage of the total NDP assemblage, and not as a percentage of the expected number of elements.

most archaeologists are faced. This leads to an important methodological question: if there is good evidence that assemblages are accumulated by humans (i.e., butchering marks or contextual information) and if the element frequency deviates from that predicted by the "natural" frequency of bones in the skeleton, how does one distinguish the effects of diverse factors such as carnivore destruction, differential transport of bones from a kill to a habitation site, differential destruction of bones by humans, differential use of bones for certain artifacts, or differential destruction of bones by mechanical and chemical weathering? A lot of attention has been devoted to separating carnivore-accumulated assemblages from human-accumulated assemblages; can one separate these and other factors operating on a single assemblage? I suggest that it is not possible to separate all such factors, because similar effects may be caused by different agencies. However, it should be possible to identify some of the sources of variation, and these are discussed below with reference to the Bonnell and Phillips assemblages.

One biasing factor in the Sierra Blanca assemblages is the way in which the assemblages were collected. Certain categories of bones are probably under-represented because they were missed during excavation: notably missing are carpals, distal ulnae, small tarsals, third phalanges, and caudal vertebrae. Because their absence is likely the result of their small size, these anatomical areas should be excluded from consideration when discussing element frequency.

A second obvious bias is the use of bone as a raw material for artifact manufacture. Bone tools from the six sites were available for analysis, and yielded some interesting results (Table 10). It is quite obvious that the representation of proximal ulnae and metatarsi in the Bonnell medium ungulate assemblage would be drastically altered by inclusion of modified bone, and low representation of the ulna or metatarsus cannot be ascribed necessarily to destruction at any of the Sierra Blanca sites.

Carnivore damage to bones and to assemblages has been an important research topic in zooarchaeology for a number of years, and virtually no assemblage is likely to be entirely free of carnivore damage. However, at the Sierra Blanca sites the degree of damage appears to be minimal. This is illustrated by considering either the entire assemblage or by considering selected elements. At Bonnell only 11 medium ungulate bones (1%) display evidence of carnivore modification in the form of punctures, pitting, furrowing, and scoring (Binford 1981:44); at Phillips 19 bones (1.2%) showed such evidence. These figures do not include carnivore damage done to bones by breaking (e.g., by spiral fractures). Still considering the entire assemblage, the frequencies of elements do not resemble element frequencies left after intensive carnivore activity. Although Binford has made extensive studies of such assemblages, Brain's work on goats in African villages (Brain 1981) is a more suitable comparison to the Sierra Blanca sites. Figure 3 compares Brain's data with Phillips and Bonnell. As Brain's quantification methods differ somewhat from mine, I have only considered long bones in the analysis. There is quite marked variation in the survival of elements in the African village, whereas this variation is less in the Sierra Blanca sites, perhaps indicating a lower intensity of carnivore activity.

TABLE 10
BONE TOOLS MADE ON IDENTIFIABLE MAMMAL ELEMENTS

Taxa	Element	Bonnell	Penasco	Phillips	Block	Hiner	Bloom
Lagomorph	Tib. Prox.	1					
Medium Ungulate	Antler	7		1		1	2
	Rib	5		1		2	
	Scapula	3			1	1	3
	Hum. Dist.	1					
	Rad. Dist.	1					
	Uln. Prox.	12	1	2			
	Uln. Shaft	6			1		
	Mc. Prox.		1				
	Tib. Dist.	1					
	Mt. Prox.	11	1			1	
	Mt. Shaft	1					
	Mt. Dist.				1		
Large Ungulate	Rib	19		6	16	11	12
	Scapula	19		1	4	2	1
	Tib. Shaft					1	

Turning to individual bones, most taphonomists note that certain bones are very susceptible to destruction by carnivores, whereas others are less susceptible. A particularly useful analysis is to compare the survival of different parts of the same bone, when these have different potentials to survive carnivore damage. Binford (1981: Figs. 5.07 and 5.08) has compared the proximal and distal humerus and the proximal and distal tibia. The humeri from Phillips and Bonnell show some destruction of the proximal end, and place the assemblage somewhere between Binford's categories of "ravaged" and "pristine." However, the tibiae yield very unusual results. The proximal tibia is approximately twice as common as the distal tibia at Phillips and Bonnell, creating a situation which is very rare in the assemblages analyzed by either Binford or Brain, both of whom consider the distal tibia a good "survivor" and proximal tibia as subject to rapid destruction. Clearly not all bones susceptible to carnivore damage were subject to heavy destruction at the Sierra Blanca sites.

As will be seen in the discussion of bone fusion and seasonality, considerable amounts of fetal or neonatal medium ungulate bone were

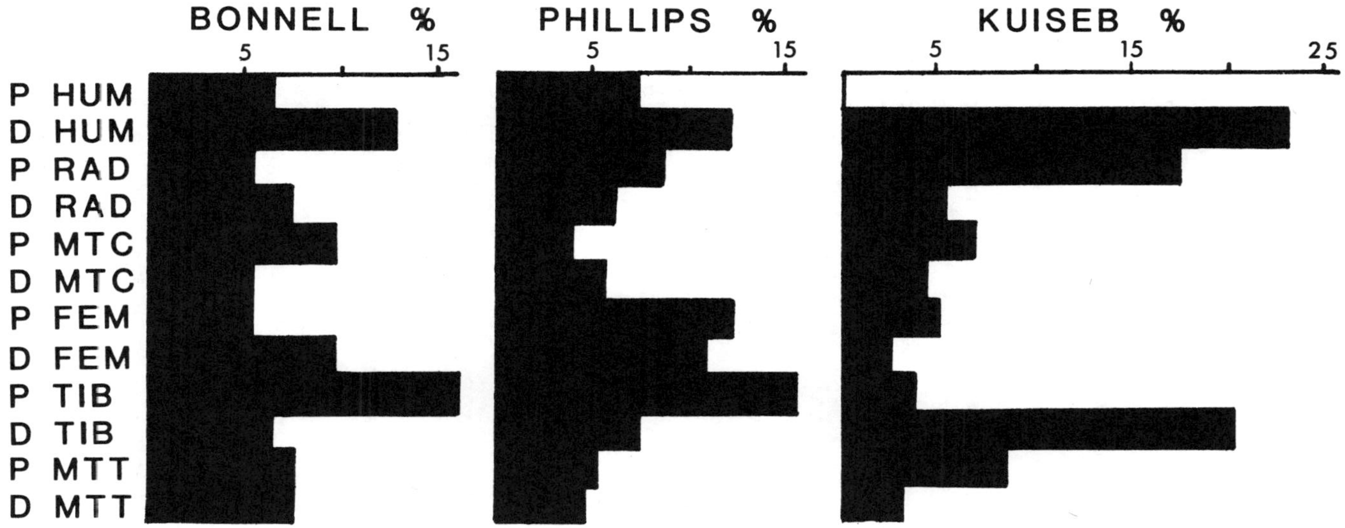

Figure 3. Element frequency (based on NDP) for selected elements of deer, antelope and medium ungulate at Bonnell and Phillips. Comparison is made to Brain's (1981) data on goats from Kuiseb.

recovered from some sites. This also suggests a lack of carnivore activity. Furthermore, it suggests that other destructive factors such as trampling, soil acidity, and pedoturbation have not seriously affected the assemblages reported here. This is confirmed by analysis of element frequency, for example the relatively high frequency of proximal humerus and the very high frequency of proximal tibia discussed above.

Although neither carnivore damage nor other damage related to bone density and survival capabilities are likely to have been a major factor in the production of element frequencies in the medium ungulate assemblages, the element frequencies do diverge from the frequencies expected in "natural" assemblages (Fig. 2). Another possible cause of this is human selection of elements for transport from a kill to the habitation sites. I will examine this by considering element frequencies within major dismemberment units identified in a cross-cultural study by Binford (1981:91-95). Excluding the head and neck areas as being too small or too highly fragmented in the assemblages reported here, three major units will be considered: trunk (thoracic vertebrae, ribs, lumbar vertebrae, sacrum, pelvis); forelimb (scapula, humerus, radius, metacarpus); and hindlimb (femur, tibia, metatarsus). It should be noted that I have not considered all elements within these major units; for example, the ulna is not considered in the forelimb, and the carpals, tarsals, sesamoids, and phalanges are excluded because of their small size. Data on the frequency of elements within the dismemberment units can be obtained from Table 9 for the Bonnell and Phillips assemblages. Other assemblages are considered too small for analysis.

Element frequency for the trunk area is described in Table 11. These data indicate that the posterior section of the vertebral column (lumbar vertebrae, sacrum, and pelvis) is over-represented when compared with the thoracic region. It is certainly possible that human butchering methods could account for this. For example, the ribcage might be removed by butchering through the ribs at their proximal and distal extremities, leaving the proximal and distal ribs and the

TABLE 11
ELEMENT FREQUENCY FOR TRUNK DISMEMBERMENT UNIT, BONNELL AND PHILLIPS ASSEMBLAGES

	Bonnell		Phillips		Natural	
Element	NDP	%	NDP	%	NDP	%
Thoracic	11	14.9	35	18.3	13	17.6
Prox. rib	15	20.3	67	35.1	26	35.1
Dist. rib	33	44.6	38	19.9	26	35.1
Lumbar	7	9.5	34	17.8	6	8.1
Sacrum	0	0	9	4.7	1	1.4
Pelvis	8	10.8	8	4.2	2	2.7
Total	74	100.1	191	100.0	74	100.0

thoracic vertebrae at the kill site. However, one should also note that the thoracic area is susceptible to more rapid destruction than the more posterior parts of the axial skeleton. For example, Binford's (1981) wolf kill data show, on the average, better survival of lumbar vertebrae and pelvis than ribs and thoracic vertebrae. Brain's diagram of a generalized bovid skeleton also indicates the higher survival potential of the posterior end of the vertebral column (Brain 1981:Fig. 148).

Data for the forelimb are summarized in Table 12. The most obvious feature of the assemblages is the decline in frequency of fragments as one moves from the proximal to the distal end of the limb. This is very unlikely to be the result of carnivore activity because quite robust bones, such as the proximal radius and proximal metacarpus exhibit low frequencies. Selective use of certain elements for bone artifacts does not seem to apply to the forelimb because relatively few forelimb elements, with the exception of the proximal ulna, were utilized for artifacts (see Table 10).

TABLE 12
ELEMENT FREQUENCY FOR FORELIMB DISMEMBERMENT UNIT, BONNELL AND PHILLIPS ASSEMBLAGES

	Bonnell		Phillips		Natural	
Element	NDP	%	NDP	%	NDP	%
Scapula	13	8.1	25	18.8	2	14.3
Prox. humerus	8	11.1	18	13.5	2	14.3
Dist. humerus	16	22.2	30	22.6	2	14.3
Prox. radius	7	9.7	21	15.8	2	14.3
Dist. radius	9	12.5	15	11.3	2	14.3
Prox. metacarpus	12	16.7	10	7.5	2	14.3
Dist. metacarpus	7	9.7	14	10.5	2	14.3
Total	72	100.0	133	100.0	14	100.1

Data for the hindlimb are presented in Table 13. As with the forelimb, the hindlimb figures show relatively low representation of the distal portion of the hindlimb. At Bonnell the situation would be somewhat different if bone tools were included in these figures, because a large number of proximal metatarsi were used as artifacts (see Table 10). However, at Phillips where the pattern is even more pronounced than at Bonnell, artifact production does not account for the low frequency of distal elements.

Thus, for both the fore- and hindlimb at Phillips and, to a lesser extent, at Bonnell there appears to be human selection for the upper part of the limbs. The concept that bones are differentially transported from kill sites to habitation or processing sites has a long history in archaeology (e.g., White 1952; Perkins and Daly 1968), and numerous authors have developed models of varying degrees of

TABLE 13
ELEMENT FREQUENCY FOR HINDLIMB DISMEMBERMENT UNIT,
BONNELL AND PHILLIPS ASSEMBLAGES

Element	Bonnell NDP	Bonnell %	Phillips NDP	Phillips %	Natural NDP	Natural %
Prox. femur	7	10.8	30	21.9	2	16.7
Dist. femur	12	18.5	27	19.7	2	16.7
Prox. tibia	20	30.8	38	27.7	2	16.7
Dist. tibia	8	12.3	18	13.1	2	16.7
Prox. metatarsus	9	13.8	13	9.5	2	16.7
Dist. metatarsus	9	13.8	11	8.0	2	16.7
Total	65	100.0	137	99.9	12	100.2

sophistication to account for this phenomenon. Almost all such models have addressed themselves largely to economic considerations, although some zooarchaeologists, notably in Europe, have been concerned with industrial or craft uses of certain skeletal elements (e.g., Chaplin 1971:138-142; Driver 1984b; Maltby 1979:11). Recent very sophisticated approaches to the analysis of element frequency have been concerned with the "value" (in nutritional terms) of different areas of the skeleton and their associated tissues. Binford (1978) has considered the "utility" of different elements in terms of the meat supported by bones and the marrow and grease contained within the bones. Speth (1983) has extended this to an archaeological situation at the Garnsey site.

We may therefore ask whether the element frequencies seen in limb bones at Bonnell and Phillips form a consistent pattern with regard to utility indices. In doing this, I am making the explicit assumption that deer and antelope anatomies are sufficiently similar to those of sheep and caribou studied by Binford (1978) to allow use of Binford's results. The most obvious correspondence between Binford's various indices of utility and the frequency of elements in the Sierra Blanca assemblages is between the standardized meat utility index (Binford 1978:19-23) and the decline in element frequency from proximal to distal limbs. There is also a good correlation between the absolute volume of the marrow cavity and the Sierra Blanca element frequency, because the upper limb bones tend to have higher volumes than lower limb bones (Binford 1978: Table 1.6). However, when one considers the quality of marrow (expressed as a high percentage of oleic acid within the fatty acids) then there is, if anything, an inverse correlation between element frequency at Bonnell and Phillips and the "value" of the elements in terms of oleic acid percentage. Finally, one should note that Binford's study of bone grease (1978:32-38) demonstrates that certain upper limb-bone ends (notably proximal humerus, proximal and distal femur, and proximal tibia) produce greater amounts of grease than most of the lower limb bones.

To summarize, limb element frequency at Bonnell and Phillips is consistent with selection for parts of the body with large quantities of meat, large marrow cavities with lower quality marrow, and with bones containing good quantities of grease. There is no suggestion that high quality marrow was particularly desired, although this does not rule out the possibility that marrow was extracted from bones at the kill site and transported back to the habitation sites. One should also note that there is little evidence for major grease-processing in the assemblages. Most long-bone ends exist as large fragments or as complete specimens; grease preparation is rendered more efficient by reduction of bones to small fragments, thus increasing the surface to volume ratio. Almost all long bones of medium ungulates from all the Sierra Blanca sites had been broken for marrow extraction, so we may presume that marrow was a desirable food. Yet it is interesting to note that of ten complete medium ungulate long bones recovered from the six Sierra Blanca assemblages, five were metapodials which should contain high quality marrow. Furthermore, if one excludes neonatal specimens from this count, then the only complete long bones from subadult or adult medium ungulates are four metapodials. If marrow quality was a factor in selection of bones for transportation to the habitation sites, one would expect that high numbers of metapodials would be present and that they would be broken. The data suggest the opposite--metapodials occur in lower frequencies than other limb bones and they are the only bones for which complete, mature specimens are known.

Thus, the data on element frequencies for limb bones at Bonnell and Phillips support an argument that when selection of body parts occurred quantity of meat and marrow was the prime consideration, and that quality of marrow was less important. This, combined with the apparent lack of intensive grease-processing, suggests that animal fat was not a major consideration in the hunting of medium ungulates. I will return to this point when discussing variation between assemblages in Sierra Blanca area sites.

Bone Modification

Cut marks presumably reflect skinning and dismemberment of animals by hunters (Binford 1981; Frison 1973), but appeared quite infrequently on the bones of medium ungulates. Location and frequency of cut marks are described in Table 14. Many of these locations are consistent with carcass disarticulation or removal of meat from bones. Those at the end of the metatarsi may be the result of removal of the phalanges from the distal end of the bone or the result of making the initial incision through the skin of the animal. Metapodials, especially metatarsi, were important elements for tool manufacture, and their removal as relatively complete units may have been desired.

Breakage of bones may result from a wide range of pre- and post-depositional processes. Considering only long bones with a "tubular" structure, it can be seen from Table 15 that about 90% of the medium ungulate bones which could be identified to element exhibit breaks of the spiral type. This suggests breakage, whether by humans or carnivores, occurred while the bone was fresh. It has been noted that "isolated articulator [sic] ends...are largely the exclusive or dominant form in assemblages cracked for marrow by man" (Binford 1981:173). Table 16 shows that at Bonnell and Phillips the dominant long-bone remnants are articular ends with less than half the shaft preserved, rather than complete long bones or long bones with one end removed. This suggests that the majority of the broken long bones in the medium ungulate assemblages were broken open for marrow by humans. Virtually all medium ungulate long bones were broken for marrow, the few exceptions being primarily fetal or neonatal specimens.

TABLE 14

LOCATION OF CUT MARKS ON MEDIUM UNGULATE BONES

Location of Cut Marks	Bonnell	Phillips	Block
Rib shaft, medial surface	2		
Rib shaft, lateral surface	4		
Sacrum, transverse process		1	
Ilium, lateral surface	2		
Ilium, ventral surface	2		
Pubis, ventral surface	1		
Humerus, distal posterior shaft		2	
Humerus, distal posterior/medial shaft	2	2	
Humerus, distal medial shaft		1	
Humerus, distal posterior/lateral shaft	1		
Radius, anterior midshaft	1		
Radius, posterior midshaft	1		
Femur, midshaft	1		
Tibia, medial/anterior proximal shaft	1		
Tibia, midshaft		1	
Metacarpus, distal posterior shaft			1
Metatarsus, distal anterior shaft		1	
Metatarsus, anterior distal condyle	1		
Metatarsus, posterior distal condyle	1		
Metatarsus, posterior distal shaft	1		
Metatarsus, distal medial and lateral shaft	1		

TABLE 15

BREAKAGE OF MEDIUM UNGULATE HUMERUS, RADIUS, FEMUR, TIBIA, METACARPUS, AND METATARSUS

	Breakage Type					
	Spiral	%	Splintered	%	Transverse	%
Bonnell	348	89.5	26	6.7	15	3.9
Phillips	351	90.2	20	5.1	18	4.6

TABLE 16
FREQUENCY OF BREAKAGE UNITS FOR MAJOR MEDIUM UNGULATE LONG BONES WITH A TUBULAR STRUCTURE

Breakage units defined in Table 1 under "long bones"

	Breakage Units				
	1	2	3	5	6
Bonnell					
Humerus	1	0	5	1	16
Radius	0	1	6	3	6
Femur	0	1	6	0	11
Tibia	0	1	13	1	7
Total	1	3	30	5	40
Phillips					
Humerus	2	0	12	0	28
Radius	2	3	16	3	7
Femur	1	0	24	0	14
Tibia	0	0	28	1	16
Total	5	3	80	4	65

Bone Fusion

Data on bone fusion are presented in Table 17. Fusion data require very large samples to be amenable for analysis (Watson 1978), and it is only at Phillips that samples are really large enough. With the exception of the very small Bloom Mound sample, all assemblages show between 20% and 36% of medium ungulate bones unfused (excluding fetal bone). The presence of fetal/neonatal bone in most assemblages denotes hunting of medium ungulates during the spring, and also attests to the qualities of preservation at the sites.

Watson (1978) has summarized many of the problems associated with the interpretation of fusion data, and has pointed out two major factors--variability in fusion age and differential destruction of bone--which prevent simple analysis of the data. Figure 4 plots for Bonnell and Phillips the percentage of fused bone for each fusion point in Table 17 against age of fusion for that point. Only fusion points for which at least seven specimens exist are considered. Age of fusion is based partly upon figures given by Lewall and Cowan (1963) for deer on good range. (No data were found for antelope.) However, in view of detailed studies of domestic and feral artiodactyl fusion (e.g., Bullock and Rackham 1982; Silver 1969), it is likely that Lewall and Cowan's scheme is oversimplified. I have therefore created four groups of fusion ages. Group I (scapula, distal humerus, proximal radius, and proximal first and second phalanges) fuse within the first eighteen months. Group II (distal tibia) fuses between 19 and 35 months. Group III (proximal ulna, distal radius, distal metacarpus, proximal femur, proximal tibia, proximal calcaneum, and distal metatarsus) fuse between 60 and 65 months. Although Lewall and Cowan include proximal humerus and distal femur with Group III, my experience suggests that these bones fuse somewhat later, and these are placed in Group IV, together with vertebrae.

TABLE 17
MEDIUM UNGULATE FUSION

f=fetal; U=unfused; F=fused; D=distal (long bones); P=proximal (long bones); A=anterior (vertebrae); P=posterior (vertebrae)

	Bonnell			Penasco		Phillips			Block			Hiner			Bloom
	f	U	F	U	F	f	U	F	f	U	F	f	U	F	F
Cervical A.			2	1	1		7	10			2			1	
Cervical P.		1	3	1	1		13	10		1					
Thoracic A.		3	3	3	1		18	16		4	5		1	4	
Thoracic P.		4	6	2			18	13		4	6		3	2	
Lumbar A.		1	3				20	14			5			1	
Lumbar P.		1	2				17	11			5				
Rib P.	4	3	8	1		6	14	46	1	1	6		2	1	
Scapula		5	7		2	2	4	19	1		3	1		2	
Hum. P.		4	4	2	1	3	11	5	1	1	5			1	
Hum. D.		4	13		1	3	1	25			8				
Rad. P.		1	6		5	1	3	19			4	1		3	
Rad. D.		2	7			2	7	6		1	2			2	
Uln. P.		3				2	3	5			1				
Uln. D.			2				1	1							
Mc. D.		4	3	1	1		3	5			5		1	1	1
Fem. P.		3	3		3	4	17	16		1	2			2	
Fem. D.		4	5	5	2	1	14	4		1			1		
Tib. P.		10	8	1	3	6	15	16	2	1				1	
Tib. D.			8	1	2	2	3	14	1	1	3		1	1	
Calc. P.		2	5		2		7	12		1				1	1
Mt. D.		6	3				4	8		1	1		1	4	
1 Phal. P.		1	18	2	3		8	56			5		1	6	
2 Phal. P.		3	18		6		3	37			3			7	
Mp. D.		3	12		1	1	23	7		2	3		1	4	

Figure 4 shows that the Phillips assemblage produces a predictable pattern of a decline of the percentage of fused bones with increasing age of fusion. This is consistent with hunting methods which kill animals over a range of age groups. Bonnell data are internally inconsistent, and almost certainly reflect a small sample rather than any unusual hunting practices.

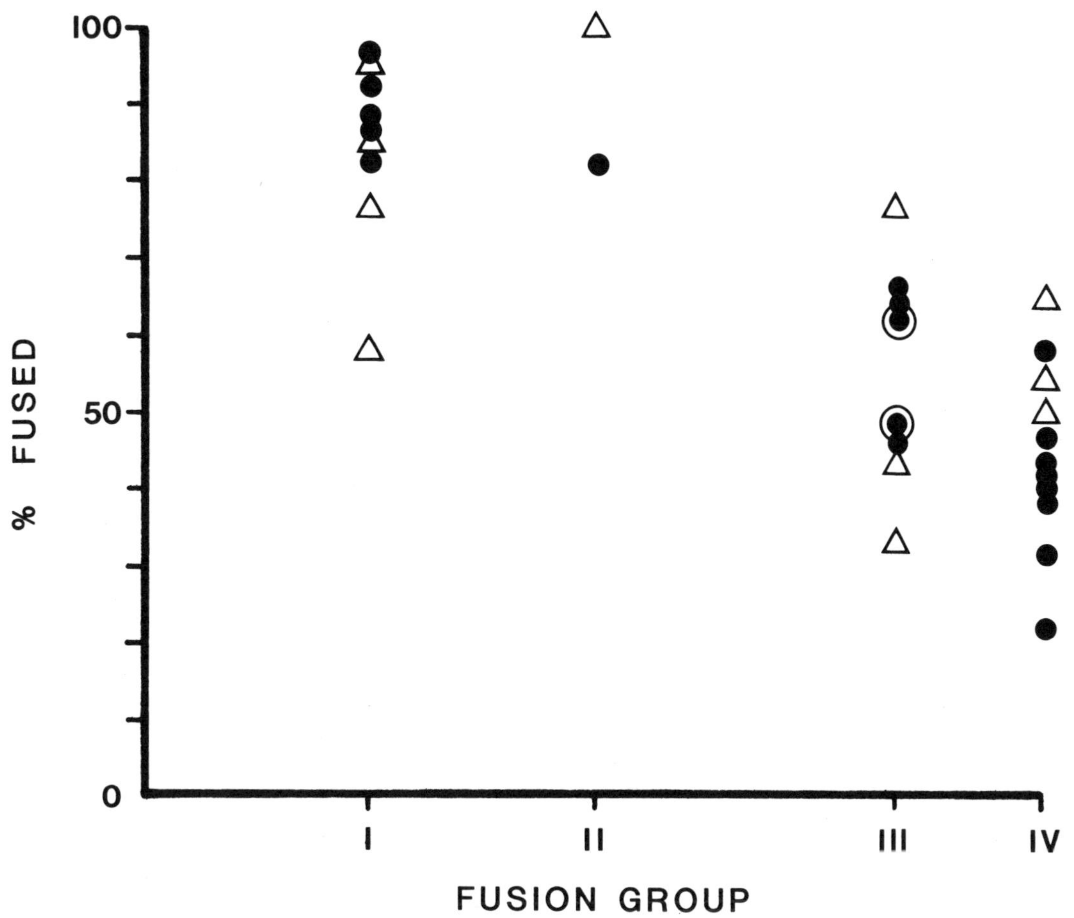

Figure 4. Bone fusion of deer, antelope, and medium ungulate at Bonnell (open triangles) and Phillips (black circles). Open circles around black circles indicate two fusion points with the same score at Phillips. Fusion groups defined in text.

Using the Phillips data, it can be seen that approximately one half of the animals were killed before reaching full skeletal maturity, and were therefore probably less than five years old at death. Phillips scapulae show that up to 20% of the animals may have been killed before reaching 15 months of age. The presence of bones classified as fetal/neonatal adds a further dimension. Considering the scapula, and including the fetal remains, 8% are fetal/neonatal, 16% were killed at less than 15 months, and 76% older than 15 months. The proximal tibia provides a maximum figure of 16% neonatal. Such data strongly emphasize the likelihood of spring hunting, a traditional pattern for antelope hunting in the Southwest (Tyler 1964).

Tooth Eruption Sequences

Only Phillips and Bonnell produced enough mandibles for analysis. At Phillips all except one are from antelope. Young animals are well represented. One mandible is from a late fetal/neonatal individual. Four mandibles show three deciduous premolars, the first molar in wear and the second molar erupting. One shows the fourth deciduous premolar still in place with the first and second molars in wear, and the third in partial wear. Finally, five show all teeth in wear, and two of these show heavy wear on the third molar. Using data supplied by Gilbert (1973), the young mandibles indicate a single fetal specimen and four animals between the ages of six weeks and 15 months. Such animals produced the unfused bones in the Group I fusion category. The sixth mandible must be around 17 months old, using Gilbert's system; it is impossible to age the last five. Thus, the small mandible sample indicates that approximately 50% of the antelope were killed when less than two years old. This is consistent with a communal hunting pattern in which a cohort is surrounded and slaughtered.

In contrast, ten mandibles and eight maxillae from Bonnell show an emphasis on mature animals. Of six deer mandibles, one is fetal/neonatal, four show all permanent teeth erupted and in wear, and a broken specimen contains the deciduous premolars. Four antelope mandibles show all permanent teeth erupted and in wear, with two of these specimens demonstrating heavy wear. Of seven deer maxillae, six show all permanent teeth in wear, and one broken specimen has heavy wear on the deciduous premolars. A single antelope maxilla is from a mature animal. Thus, of the ten mandibles of deer and antelope, the only dentally immature specimens are a fetal/neonatal individual and a broken specimen.

The Large Ungulate Assemblage

Element Frequency

Large ungulates diverge in major respects from the expected element frequency distribution. Large ungulate and *Bison* NISP data are summarized in Table 18 and NDP in Table 19.

TABLE 18
LARGE UNGULATE AND BISON NISP

	Bonnell	Penasco	Phillips	Block	Hiner	Bloom
Mandible			1			
Cervical	2		5	3		
Thoracic	16		6	4	1	
Lumbar	1		3	4		
Vertebrae Unc.	2					
Rib Prox.	8		7	10		
Rib Dist.	5		4	8		
Rib Shaft	281	2	132	127	25	
Costal Cart.	7		12	13	2	
Scapula					2	
Hum. Prox.	1			3		1
Hum. Dist.						1
Hum. Shaft	4			6	1	
Rad. Whole						1
Rad. Prox.	1					
Uln. Whole				1		
Uln. Prox.				1		
Uln. Shaft						1
Mc. Prox.			1			
Pelvis						2
Fem. Prox.	1			4		
Fem. Shaft	4		1	4	1	
Patella						1
Tib. Prox.				1		
Tib. Dist.						1
Tib. Shaft	4		4	2	1	1
Total	337	2	176	191	33	9

Here is a clear picture of element selectivity on the part of the humans. All assemblages, except Bloom Mound, are dominated by elements from the vertebral column and ribcage. This is particularly apparent when NISP is considered, because of the very large number of rib shaft fragments recovered from some sites. However, it is also true for the NDP quantification method which only considers proximal and distal ends of ribs, and does not count rib shafts. There is no likelihood that such element frequencies could be produced by any type of differential preservation because it is the most fragile areas of the skeleton that are being preserved. Speth's recent study of the Garnsey bison kill (Speth 1983) shows that ribs were removed in large numbers from the kill. It is quite possible that sections of ribcage were either traded to the Sierra Blanca region by bison hunters farther east or that the occupants of the Sierra Blanca sites participated in bison kills. Spielmann (1983) has reviewed the evidence for Plains-Southwest contact, and suggests that trade in the period A.D. 1250 to 1450 was characterized by small-scale down-the-line exchange (Spielmann

1983:268) between central New Mexico and the Plains. Data from the Sierra Blanca villages would suggest an intermediate position in this system. Most of the bison bone reaching pueblos in central New Mexico apparently arrived in the form of artifacts or ritual paraphernalia (Spielmann 1983). However, while bison bone artifacts are present at the Sierra Blanca sites, their inhabitants were also receiving quantities of bison meat, some still presumably attached to the bone. It is therefore quite likely that the exchange of subsistence products postulated by Spielmann took place in the Sierra Blanca area. Whether or not the Sierra Blanca inhabitants acted as intermediaries between the Plains and villages farther to the west remains to be studied.

TABLE 19

LARGE UNGULATE AND BISON NDP

	Bonnell	Penasco	Phillips	Block	Hiner	Bloom
Mandible			1			
Cervical			2	2		
Thoracic			2	1		
Lumbar				1		
Rib Prox.	8		7	10		
Rib Dist.	5		4	8		
Hum. Prox.	1			3		1
Rad. Prox.	1					1
Rad. Dist.						1
Uln. Prox.				2		
Uln. Dist.				1		
Mc. Prox.			1			
Fem. Prox.	1			4		
Tib. Prox.				1		
Tib. Dist.						1

Bone Modification

The only evidence for cut marks was recorded on the Bonnell ribs. Four specimens showed light cuts on the medial surface, and 14 specimens had cuts on the lateral surface. Ribs were frequently broken below the head in all assemblages, and were generally broken into pieces along the shaft, possibly to facilitate boiling in a pot.

The presence of transverse processes and neural spines in the samples is reflected in the relatively high NISP figures for vertebrae. These bones may have arrived at the sites in association with cuts of meat such as the hump or the tenderloin.

3
INTER-ASSEMBLAGE COMPARISONS

The six assemblages (Tables 20 to 25) display a predictable pattern of increasing species diversity with increased sample size. Even though the Bonnell assemblage contains a much greater variety of taxa than other assemblages, this should not be considered as indicative of different patterns of animal exploitation; instead, it is likely to be a simple effect of sample size.

The majority of taxa are either intrusive to the cultural deposits or, at best, have an obscure taphonomic history. Important variation between assemblages is that which occurs when the major hunted taxa are considered. In this section of the analysis I will consider *Sylvilagus*, *Lepus*, *Odocoileus*, *Antilocapra*, medium ungulate, *Bison*, and large ungulate. Data for these classes are summarized in Tables 26 and 27.

Regardless of which quantification method is used, there are differences in the relative frequencies of major groupings (lagomorphs, all medium ungulates, and all large ungulates), and differences in relative frequencies between taxa within these groupings (i.e., *Sylvilagus* versus *Lepus*, and *Odocoileus* versus *Antilocapra*). Excluding Bloom Mound, because of small sample size and poor preservation, one can define two types of assemblage. Phillips, Block Lookout, and Hiner show relatively high percentages of all medium ungulates, and relatively low percentages of lagomorphs. Bonnell and Penasco reverse this position, with considerably reduced medium ungulate frequencies and higher frequencies of lagomorphs. Large ungulates are rare at most sites, especially when the NDP quantification technique is employed. Only Block Lookout contains a significant quantity of large ungulates in the NDP assemblage. Within the major groups there is no clear variation for lagomorph species. Generally, as in many sites in the eastern part of the Southwest, cottontails outnumber jackrabbits. Penasco is the only site where the two taxa occur in approximately equal numbers. For the medium ungulates, there is considerable variation between deer and antelope. Penasco and Bonnell contain more deer than antelope, while at Phillips, Block Lookout, and Hiner medium ungulate assemblages are dominated by antelope.

These variations have been noted previously (Driver 1984a) and referred to different ecological conditions in the catchment areas of the sites. I also suggested that variation in agricultural intensity might affect the type of hunting undertaken from the different sites. Recently, Speth and Scott (1983, 1984, 1985) have proposed that data from Kelley's excavations support a contention derived from their work at the Angus site that there was a change in emphasis from small mammal to large mammal hunting in the Sierra Blanca region. Before contrasting these two opposing positions, it is worth noting that neither I nor

TABLE 20
BONNELL FAUNAL ASSEMBLAGE

See Appendix for detailed descriptions

Taxa	NISP	%	NDP	%	MNI	%
Sylvilagus	1036	29.3	992	39.6	89	40.3
Lepus	250	7.1	228	9.1	15	6.8
Spermophilus	33	0.9	33	1.3	19	8.6
Cynomys	81	2.3	81	3.2	34	15.4
Large sciurid	329	9.3	377	15.1		
Thomomys	82	2.3	85	3.4	31	14.0
Peromyscus	2	0.06	2	0.08	1	0.5
Neotoma	9	0.3	9	0.4	5	2.3
Ondatra zibethicus	17	0.5	18	0.7	4	1.8
Microtus	2	0.06	2	0.08	1	0.5
Erethizon dorsatum	1	0.03	1	0.04	1	0.5
Small rodent	137	3.9	169	6.7		
Canis	25	0.7	24	1.0	2	0.9
Urocyon cinereoargenteus	3	0.08	2	0.08	1	0.5
Fox	15	0.4	13	0.5	2	0.9
Ursus	1	0.03			1	0.5
Mustela frenata	1	0.03	1	0.04	1	0.5
Mephitis mephitis	9	0.3	10	0.4	2	0.9
Felis concolor	4	0.1	7	0.3	1	0.5
Lynx rufus	3	0.08	3	0.1	1	0.5
Odocoileus	152	4.3	150	6.0	4	1.8
Antilocapra americana	82	2.3	85	3.4	4	1.8
Medium ungulate	92	26.1	196	7.8		
Bison	47	1.3	16	0.6	2	0.9
Large ungulate	290	8.2				
Small mammal	401		18			
Medium mammal	1656					
Large mammal	153					
Unidentified	82					
Total	5826		2522		221	
Identified total	3534	99.97	2504	99.32	221	100.4

TABLE 21
PENASCO FAUNAL ASSEMBLAGE

See Appendix for detailed descriptions

Taxa	NISP	%	NDP	%	MNI	%
Sylvilagus	48	15.3	46	20.3	9	30.0
Lepus	56	17.8	47	20.7	5	16.7
Cynomys	8	2.5	7	3.1	3	10.0
Large sciurid	9	2.9	8	3.5		
Thomomys	4	1.3	4	1.8	2	6.7
Ondatra zibethicus	14	4.5	12	5.3	4	13.3
Small rodent	14	4.5	8	3.5		
Mephitis mephitis	2	0.6	2	0.9	1	3.3
Lynx	1	0.3	1	0.4	1	3.3
Odocoileus	56	17.8	57	25.1	3	10.0
Antilocapra americana	9	2.9	11	4.8	2	6.7
Medium ungulate	91	29.0	24	10.6		
Large ungulate	2	0.6				
Small mammal	25					
Medium mammal	109					
Large mammal	2					
Total	450		227		30	
Identified total	314	100.0	227	100.0	30	100.0

TABLE 22
PHILLIPS FAUNAL ASSEMBLAGE

See Appendix for detailed descriptions

Taxa	NISP	%	NDP	%	MNI	%
Sylvilagus	158	7.8	154	12.6	18	26.9
Lepus	51	2.5	55	4.5	4	6.0
Cynomys	21	1.0	19	1.6	11	16.4
Large sciurid	72	3.5	94	7.7	9	13.4
Thomomys	5	0.2	2	0.2	2	3.0
Canis	7	0.3	11	0.9	1	1.5
Vulpes macrotis	1	0.05	1	0.08	1	1.5
Taxidea taxus	2	1.0	2	0.2	1	1.5
Felis concolor	1	0.05	2	0.2	1	1.5
Lynx	3	0.1	3	0.2	1	1.5
Odocoileus	100	4.9	97	7.9	5	7.5
Antilocapra americana	333	16.4	392	32.1	12	17.9
Medium ungulate	1099	54.2	374	30.6		
Bison	32	1.6	17	1.4	1	1.5
Large ungulate	144	7.1				
Small mammal	35					
Medium mammal	795					
Large mammal	30					
Total	2889		1223		67	
Identified total	2029	100.7	1223	100.18	67	100.1

TABLE 23
BLOCK LOOKOUT FAUNAL ASSEMBLAGE

See Appendix for detailed descriptions

Taxa	NISP	%	NDP	%	MNI	%
Sylvilagus	25	4.8	26	12.9	5	26.3
Lepus	9	1.7	7	3.5	2	10.5
Large sciurid	2	0.4	3	1.5	1	5.3
Canis	2	0.4	1	0.5	1	5.3
Lynx	2	0.4	3	1.5	1	5.3
Neotoma	1	0.2	1	0.5	1	5.3
Odocoileus	18	3.5	13	6.4	1	5.3
Antilocapra americana	60	11.6	66	32.7	4	21.1
Medium ungulate	207	40.0	49	24.3		
Bison	22	4.3	11	5.5	3	15.8
Large ungulate	169	32.7	22	10.9		
Small mammal	20		3			
Medium mammal	163					
Large mammal	70					
Total	770		205		19	
Identified total	517	100.0	202	100.2	19	100.2

TABLE 24
HINER FAUNAL ASSEMBLAGE

See Appendix for detailed descriptions

Taxa	NISP	%	NDP	%	MNI	%
Sylvilagus	9	4.2	12	12.1	3	25.0
Lepus	6	2.8	4	4.0	2	16.7
Thomomys	1	0.5	1	1.0	1	8.3
Canis	2	0.9	1	1.0	1	8.3
Odocoileus	6	2.8	6	6.1	1	8.3
Antilocapra americana	47	22.2	51	51.5	3	25.0
Medium ungulate	108	50.9	24	24.2		
Bison	6	2.8			1	8.3
Large ungulate	27	12.7				
Small mammal	19					
Medium mammal	53					
Large mammal	5					
Total	289		99		12	
Identified total	212	99.8	99	99.9	12	99.9

TABLE 25
BLOOM MOUND FAUNAL ASSEMBLAGE

See Appendix for detailed descriptions

Taxa	NISP	%	NDP	%	MNI	%
Sylvilagus	7	18.4	6	23.1	2	25.0
Lepus	3	7.9	2	7.7	1	12.5
Large sciurid	5	13.2	7	26.9	1	12.5
Canis	3	7.9	2	7.7	1	12.5
Odocoileus	6	15.8			1	12.5
Antilocapra americana	2	5.3	2	7.7	1	12.5
Medium ungulate	3	7.9	1	3.8		
Bison	9	23.7	6	23.1	1	12.5
Small mammal	2					
Medium mammal	47					
Large mammal	17					
Total	104		26		8	
Identified total	38	100.1	26	100.0	8	100.0

TABLE 26
NISP DATA FOR MAJOR TAXONOMIC GROUPS

Taxa	Bonnell	%	Penasco	%	Phillips	%	Block	%	Hiner	%	Bloom	%
Sylvilagus	1036	37.3	48	18.3	158	8.2	25	4.9	9	4.3	7	23.3
Lepus	250	9.0	56	21.4	51	2.7	9	1.8	6	2.9	3	10.0
Odocoileus	152	5.5	56	21.4	100	5.2	18	3.5	6	2.9	6	20.0
Antilocapra	82	2.9	9	3.4	333	17.4	60	11.8	47	22.5	2	6.7
Medium ungulate	923	33.2	91	34.7	1099	57.3	207	40.6	108	51.7	3	10.0
Bison	47	1.7	0	0	32	1.7	22	4.3	6	2.9	9	30.0
Large ungulate	290	10.4	2	0.8	144	7.5	169	33.1	27	12.9	0	
Total	2780	100.0	262	100.0	1917	100.0	510	100.0	209	100.1	30	100.0
All lagomorph	1286	46.3	104	39.7	209	10.9	34	6.7	15	7.2	10	33.3
All medium ungulate	1157	41.6	156	59.5	1532	79.9	285	55.9	161	77.0	11	36.7
All large ungulate	337	12.1	2	0.8	176	9.2	191	37.5	33	15.8	9	30.0

TABLE 27
NDP DATA FOR MAJOR TAXONOMIC GROUPS

Taxa	Bonnell	%	Penasco	%	Phillips	%	Block	%	Hiner	%	Bloom	%
Sylvilagus	992	59.5	46	24.9	154	14.1	26	13.4	12	12.4	6	11.8
Lepus	228	13.7	47	25.4	55	5.1	7	3.6	4	4.1	2	1.8
Odocoileus	150	9.0	57	30.8	97	8.9	13	6.7	6	6.2	0	
Antilocapra	85	5.1	11	5.9	392	36.0	66	34.0	51	52.5	2	11.8
Medium ungulate	196	11.8	24	13.0	374	34.3	49	25.3	24	24.7	1	5.9
Bison	16	1.0	0		17	1.6	11	5.7	0		6	35.3
Large ungulate	0		0		0		22	11.3	0		0	
Total	1667	100.1	185	100.0	1089	100.0	194	100.0	97	99.9	17	100.1
All lagomorph	1220	73.2	93	50.2	209	19.2	33	17.0	16	16.5	8	47.1
All medium ungulate	431	25.9	92	49.7	863	79.2	128	66.0	81	83.5	3	17.6
All large ungulate	16	1.0	0		17	1.6	33	17.0	0		6	35.3

Speth and Scott have provided an exhaustive evaluation of hypotheses to account for inter-assemblage variation in the Sierra Blanca. The following hypotheses might account for the observed differences in the faunas at the five sites excavated by Kelley and at the Angus site.

1. The physical position of the sites within local ecosystems may influence the type and quantities of animals hunted.

2. As suggested by Speth and Scott, the utilization of mammals in the Sierra Blanca region changes through time in response to changing human aggregation and economic patterns.

3. Variation in agricultural systems from one area to another may affect hunting systems, as suggested previously (Driver 1984a).

This list of hypotheses excludes climatic, technological, and demographic change as important factors. These have been reviewed by Speth and Scott (1983), following the work of Bayham (1982). I agree with Speth and Scott that there is no good evidence for the influence of such factors in the Sierra Blanca region at the time period under discussion. Thus, discussion of inter-assemblage variation is reduced to a question of spatial variation versus temporal change. My previously expressed view is that the differences are due to some form of spatial variation in either natural resources or human agricultural systems; Speth and Scott perceive the differences as due to change in the socioeconomic system through time.

Analysis of temporal change requires good temporal control, and there is considerable doubt that such control exists for the assemblages under study. Speth and Scott base their documentation of change through time on (a) two assemblages from different time periods at the Angus site, and (b) arrangement of the Kelley assemblages into a time sequence. While I cannot comment in detail upon the Angus site, it is worth noting that the assemblages are drawn from two different areas. The early assemblage is from a group of pit rooms, while the later is from above-ground structures. Speth and Scott do not present evidence that the fill of these two areas dates to the periods under question, even though their dating of the sequence of construction is presumably correct. Furthermore, even if the dates for the assemblages are correct, assemblage sizes are very different. The early period assemblage contains over 4000 bones, while the later contains about 330. In terms of identifiable specimens, the later assemblage contains only 124 identified mammal bones, of which only 58 are identified to the genus or family level. One should also note that Speth and Scott do not distinguish between food and nonfood items, nor do they consider the possibility of intrusive specimens.

With regard to the chronological position of the assemblages recovered from sites excavated by Holden and Kelley, I believe it is difficult to assess the extent to which an accurate sequence can be reconstructed. Speth and Scott (1984, 1985) have excluded the Bonnell site from their analysis, although it was included in their initial statement (1983). This is appropriate, given the long occupation of the Bonnell site and the difficulties inherent in trying to subdivide the Bonnell assemblage recovered thirty years ago. However, Speth and Scott retain a "sequence" of assemblages from the Sierra Blanca region with which I disagree. Their proposed sequence states that Penasco (Glencoe Phase) is earlier than Phillips (Corona-Lincoln Phase), Block Lookout, and Hiner (both Lincoln Phase). As has been stated elsewhere, the Glencoe Phase in the south of the Sierra Blanca region overlaps chronologically with the Corona and Lincoln Phases in the north of the region (Kelley 1966; Wiseman 1983). One cannot assume that the Penasco site is necessarily earlier than Lincoln Phase sites. On the basis of evidence presented by Kelley (1966), the case for producing a chronological sequence of faunal assemblages is weak.

Even if sites could be arranged in a temporal sequence, it is possible to provide alternative explanations for the variation observed in assemblages from sites reported in this study and from the Angus site. One alternative view is that the location of sites has an important effect upon hunting and other economic activities undertaken at that site. The theoretical basis for this approach has a long history in archaeology, commencing at least as early as Fox's (1923) regional study and continuing in the British school to site catchment analysis (e.g., Higgs and Vita-Finzi 1970) and its variants (e.g., Foley 1977). In North America the locational approach has never enjoyed the popularity it achieved in Europe, even though site catchment analysis in various forms has been applied to North American problems. There are a number of reasons for this. First, the initial formulation of site catchment analysis by Higgs was couched in extremely deterministic language (e.g., Higgs and Jarman 1975:2). Second, locational analysis is most productive when applied to sedentary cultures, whereas much of North American archaeology is concerned with mobile groups. North American archaeologists have made frequent incursions to ecology or cultural ecology for models of human behavior which tend to emphasize movement from one patch or resource to another rather than consider the totality of environment around any one site (e.g., Jochim 1976; Winterhalder and Smith 1981).

Nevertheless, site catchment can be a valuable theoretical basis for initial formulation of human use of the environment in a sedentary culture. The theoretical basis of my analysis of the composition of the Sierra Blanca faunal assemblages begins with the assumption that humans habitually exploit certain areas around permanently occupied habitation sites. The faunal remains found in a village are likely to reflect the available habitats and animal populations around the site. The assemblages do not, of course, provide a representative sample of such habitats and populations; rather they should be considered as providing ordinal data on habitat or species availability. There are numerous caveats which could be applied to this theoretical position. For example, long-range hunting expeditions will introduce species from habitats at some distance from the site; changes in human population levels may result in the utilization of new resources or extinction of old resources; environmental change may necessitate a restructuring of subsistence patterns. Regardless of these problems in applying locational models, one should surely investigate the role of local habitats in structuring faunal composition at sites in the Sierra Blanca region. Speth and Scott have not considered this approach, but it provides a theoretical alternative to their model of diachronic change. It is important to note that Speth and Scott's documentation of change is based upon sites from different areas of the Sierra Blanca region. Thus, they have held the environment as a constant throughout the region. I propose that spatial variation within the overall Upper Sonoran vegetation of the Sierra Blanca region requires investigation, and that it may support different hypotheses about the causes of inter-assemblage variation.

In order to compare assemblages, I will consider the data from sites reported in this study as well as data from the Angus site (Speth and Scott 1983, 1984, 1985). I will use NISP as the basis for comparison, because this quantification method is common, and will confine analysis to the taxa which were major subsistence items and which probably owe their origin on the sites to human predation. Angus NISP data are presented in Table 28. The relative frequencies of three major classes of mammals--lagomorphs, all medium-sized ungulates, and all large ungulates--are plotted in Figure 5 for five of Kelley's sites and the two Angus site assemblages. Both Angus faunas fall in the same group as Bonnell and Penasco, and are clearly differentiated from the Lincoln Phase sites. Further similarities between Angus and Bonnell and Penasco are evident when one considers the relationship between deer, antelope, and lagomorphs. As noted above, the northern Lincoln Phase sites show low values for lagomorphs and a high antelope-to-deer ratio. The southern Glencoe sites have a high value for lagomorphs and a low antelope to deer ratio. This relationship also holds at Angus, as can be seen from Figure 6.

The extent to which sites of the Lincoln Phase are unusual is demonstrated by considering assemblages from other parts of New Mexico. Data presented by Young (1980) for Tijeras Pueblo, San Antonio, and Coconito all fall closer to the Sierra Blanca sites of the Glencoe area than they do to Sierra Blanca sites of the Lincoln Phase area (Fig. 5). Furthermore, the deer/antelope/lagomorph relationship is also more similar to Glencoe Phase than Lincoln Phase sites (Fig. 6).

All of the foregoing discussion is based upon the premise that lagomorphs, medium ungulates, and large ungulates were the major consumed species at the Sierra Blanca sites. Although I have presented evidence to the contrary, it could be argued that other species, notably the large sciurids, were also consumed. Although my analysis suggests that this is unlikely, if the large sciurids are included as a dietary item, there is still clear separation between Bonnell, Penasco, and the two phases at Angus on the one hand, and the three more northerly sites of Phillips, Block, and Hiner on the other.

TABLE 28
SELECTED NISP DATA FROM THE ANGUS SITE

[Speth and Scott 1983]

	Early		Late	
	NISP	%	NISP	%
Sylvilagus	495	42.3	14	27.5
Lepus	142	12.1	5	9.8
Odocoileus	404	34.5	25	49.0
Antilocapra	3	0.3	0	0
Ovis	6	0.5	1	2.0
Medium ungulate	70	6.0	0	0
Bison	15	1.3	1	2.0
Large ungulate	36	3.1	5	9.8
Total	1171	100.1	51	100.1
All lagomorph	637	54.4	19	37.3
All medium ungulate	449	38.3	26	51.0
All large ungulate	85	7.3	6	11.8

It would appear that the three Lincoln Phase assemblages are anomalous, not only at a regional scale, but also extra-regionally. I propose that such well defined spatial variation is not the result of change through time but rather that it results from differences in local environments around the various sites.

The two major variables in environment within the Upper Sonoran vegetation zone are topography and water availability, and these find their most obvious expression in vegetation communities. Detailed vegetation maps of the Sierra Blanca region are not available, but I have visited Bonnell, Phillips, Block Lookout, and Angus, and have observed the area of the Hiner site, although not the site itself. I have not visited Penasco. All of these sites require a detailed site catchment analysis, but this is not possible in many cases because of problems in gaining access to private land. Topography around these sites may be obtained by consulting maps. When one considers vegetation and topography, significant differences emerge, and these are summarized below.

One group of sites--Bonnell, Penasco, and Angus--are located close to permanent watercourses which emerge in the Sacramento Mountains and flow east through heavily dissected topography. That these were permanent watercourses in the past is suggested by the presence of muskrat at all three sites. The topography within a 10 km radius of each site can be described as dissected, and consists of steep slopes with numerous canyons, valleys, and arroyos. Each site lies on a major valley which cuts through the dissected topography and provides areas of relatively flat river bottoms and associated terraces. The vegetation around Bonnell and Angus reflects their position in these

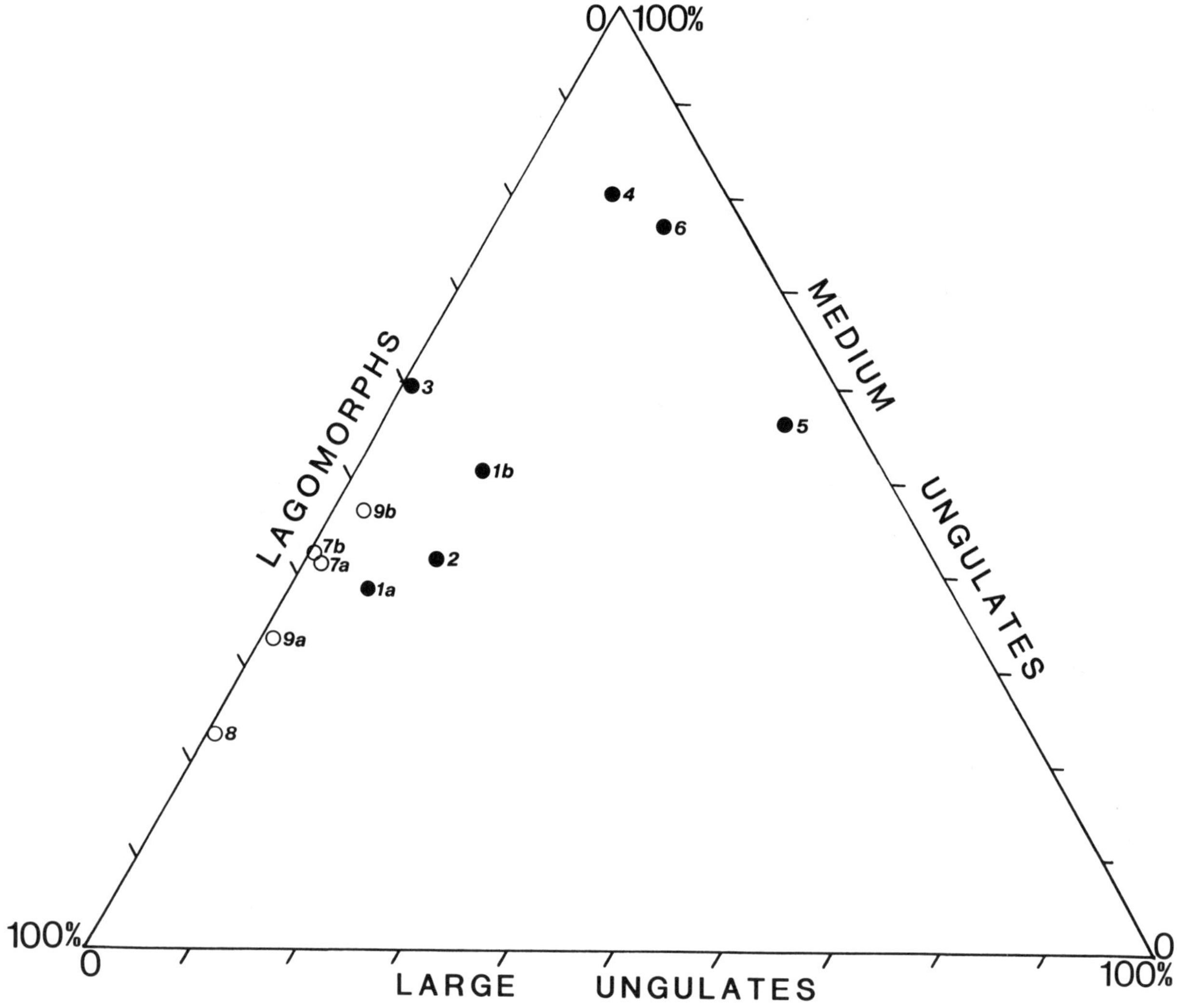

Figure 5. Percentages of all lagomorphs, all medium ungulates (deer, antelope, and medium ungulate), and all large ungulates (bison and large ungulate), based on NISP. Black circles=Sierra Blanca sites; open circles=other sites. 1=Angus Early (a) and Late (b); 2=Bonnell; 3=Penasco; 4=Phillips; 5=Block Lookout; 6=Hiner; 7=Tijeras Early (a) and Late (b); 8=Coconito; 9=San Antonio Middle (a) and Late (b). Data for sites 7 to 9 from Young (1980).

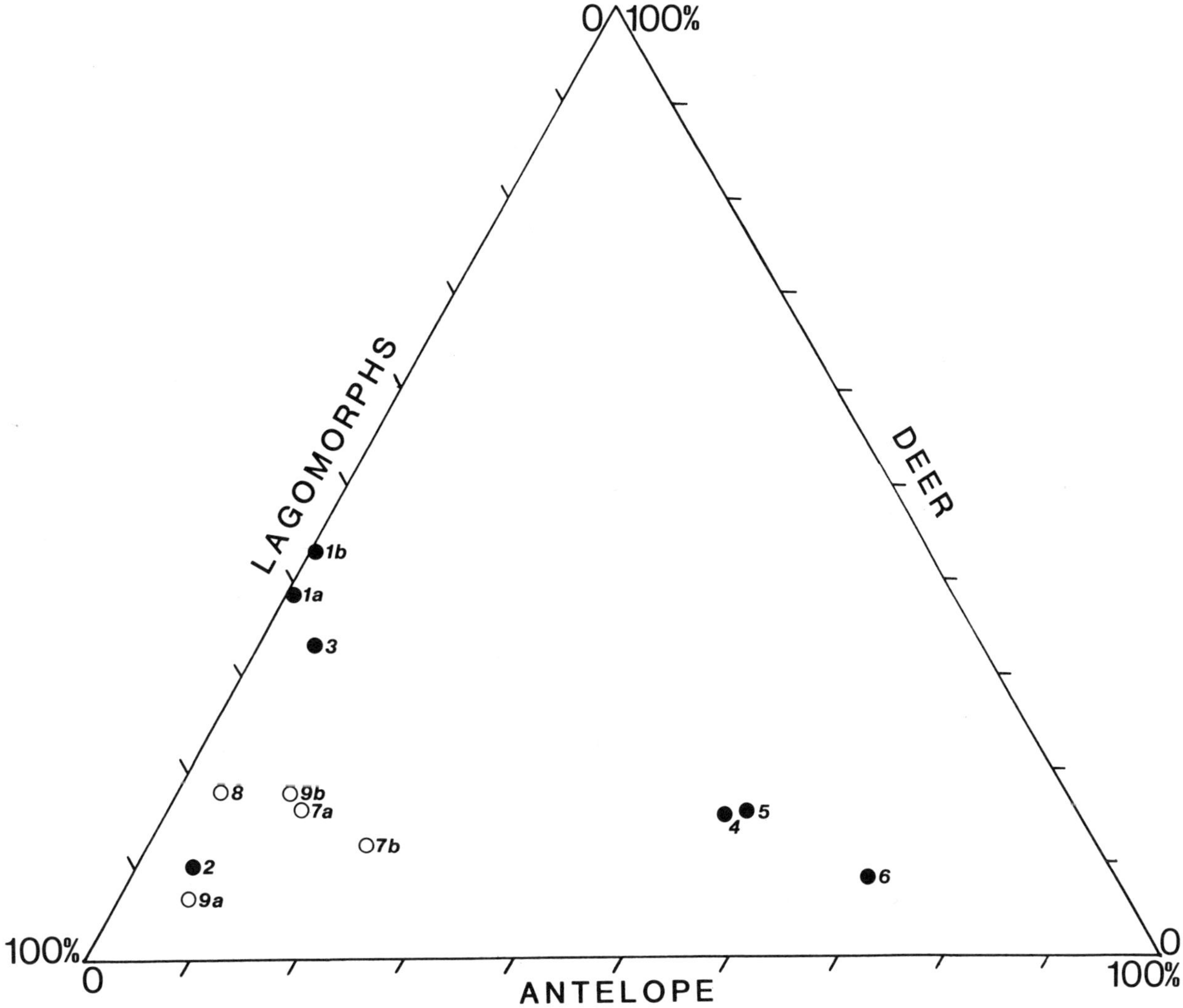

Figure 6. Percentages of all lagomorphs, deer, and antelope, based on NISP. See Figure 5 for key.

valleys and also their relationship to the Sacramento Mountains. The Rio Bonito and Rio Ruidoso support a vegetation unlike that found in most of the Sierra Blanca region. Cottonwoods (*Populus*), willows (*Salix*), Russian olive (*Oleagnus angustifolia*), and walnut (*Juglans major*) are present, together with other species of the Upper Sonoran zone such as piñon (*Pinus edulis*) and juniper (*Juniperus*). A variety of shrubs contribute to a dense underbrush along the course of the rivers. Away from the rivers the vegetation depends largely upon elevation. Around the Bonnell site piñon and various junipers are common on the mountains. Angus, at a slightly higher elevation and receiving a greater precipitation as a result of the proximity of the Sierra Blanca Mountains, includes oak/piñon/juniper and fir/pine associations within 10 km of the site.

A second group of sites--Phillips, Block Lookout, and Hiner--are situated within very different environmental conditions, although still within the Upper Sonoran zone. Topographically, the major feature of all three sites is the presence of extensive flat to undulating plains within a 10 km radius of the site. These plains, which lie north of Capitan Mountain and east of the Sacramentos, support a grassland dominated by grama (*Bouteloua*). The plains are relatively undissected, although arroyo systems do provide some relief. Hiner is well out in the plains, but both Phillips and Block Lookout are located quite close to mountains. The vegetation within a 10 km radius of these three sites is a mixture of grassland on the plains and dry piñon/juniper forests on the mountain slopes.

Transects across the topographic features within a 10 km radius of the sites are provided in Figure 7. As can be seen, absolute changes in elevation are high at Phillips, Block Lookout, and Angus, all of which lie close to major mountain ranges. At the other three sites absolute variation is small. However, the three sites north of Capitan Mountain--Phillips, Block Lookout, and Hiner--are characterized by areas of flat relief. In the case of Hiner, most of the catchment area consists of flat plains supporting a grassland vegetation. Phillips and Block Lookout catchments include either flat plains or steep slopes of major mountains. This can be contrasted with Angus, Bonnell, and Penasco where the topography is noticeably dissected, with frequent minor changes in elevation.

It can be suggested that the differences in the antelope to deer ratio at the six sites are the result of environmental differences. At the local level, position of the three southern sites--Bonnell, Penasco, and Angus--in valley bottoms with permanent water should encourage hunting of deer, which are much more likely than antelope to inhabit such areas. At a larger scale, the 10 km catchment of the southern sites includes numerous areas of broken and dissected terrain, often supporting areas of dry forest or woodland. Again, this is deer, rather than antelope, habitat. The three northern sites--Hiner, Block Lookout, and Phillips--contain varying areas of flat grassland within their 10 km radius, but the latter two also have access to deer habitat on the forested slopes of the mountains. It is interesting to note that as sites recede from the grasslands the ratio of antelope to deer declines. The highest antelope to deer ratio is about 6:1 at Hiner, which lies well within the grassland environment. Phillips and Block Lookout are at the edge of the grasslands, and the ratio is about 3:1. Moving south of the Capitan Mountains, Bonnell has a ratio of 1:2 and Penasco 1:6. Angus, which lies farthest from the grasslands and most deeply in forested mountain regions has a ratio of about 1:100.

The other major difference between the northern and southern sites is their degree of reliance on lagomorphs, notably *Sylvilagus*. From Bailey's (1931) account it is apparent that cottontails favor well-vegetated areas with shrubs and trees rather than open grasslands. I would suspect that cottontails were more abundant in the broken wooded country associated with the area south of the Capitan Mountains. Surprisingly, there is no increase in jackrabbits relative to cottontails in the northern sites, even though jackrabbits should be common on the grasslands, as they certainly are today. The reasons for this will be discussed later.

One should note that the increase in medium ungulates over lagomorphs at the northern sites is almost entirely due to the presence of antelope. Ratios of deer to lagomorphs are very similar at all sites except Bonnell, where there is a superabundance of cottontails. Thus, to a large extent, the differences between the assemblages are due to the presence or absence of antelope hunting. Examination of Figure 6 demonstrates that antelope in the Sierra Blanca region is either greater than 50% of the lagomorph/deer/antelope assemblage or around 5%. Consequently, high frequencies of all medium ungulates in Figure 5 are the result of high antelope frequencies. It can be hypothesized, although not demonstrated, that the changes in the importance of antelope are due to communal hunting in the north and individual stalking in the south. Demonstration of these two hunting methods is not possible on the basis of the current faunal assemblages, but it might help explain the sharp differentiation in the amount of antelope between the two areas.

Although one can postulate that variation in the faunal assemblages is the result of different hunting strategies in different environments, one must also consider the interrelationship between hunting and agriculture. Zooarchaeologists deal (at best) with relative data. One cannot determine the extent to which meat contributed to the total diet of the prehistoric Sierra Blanca inhabitants, nor can one determine whether a change in relative frequency of species represents a change in the absolute use of a particular meat source. An analog to this problem is well known in palynology, where relative pollen diagrams are usually studied in conjunction with "absolute" or influx diagrams (e.g., Maher 1972). The two types of assemblage in the Sierra Blanca have been defined in relative terms. The fact that antelope is more frequent in the Lincoln Phase sites than the Glencoe Phase sites may mean one of two things: either the *per capita* meat consumption of Lincoln Phase people

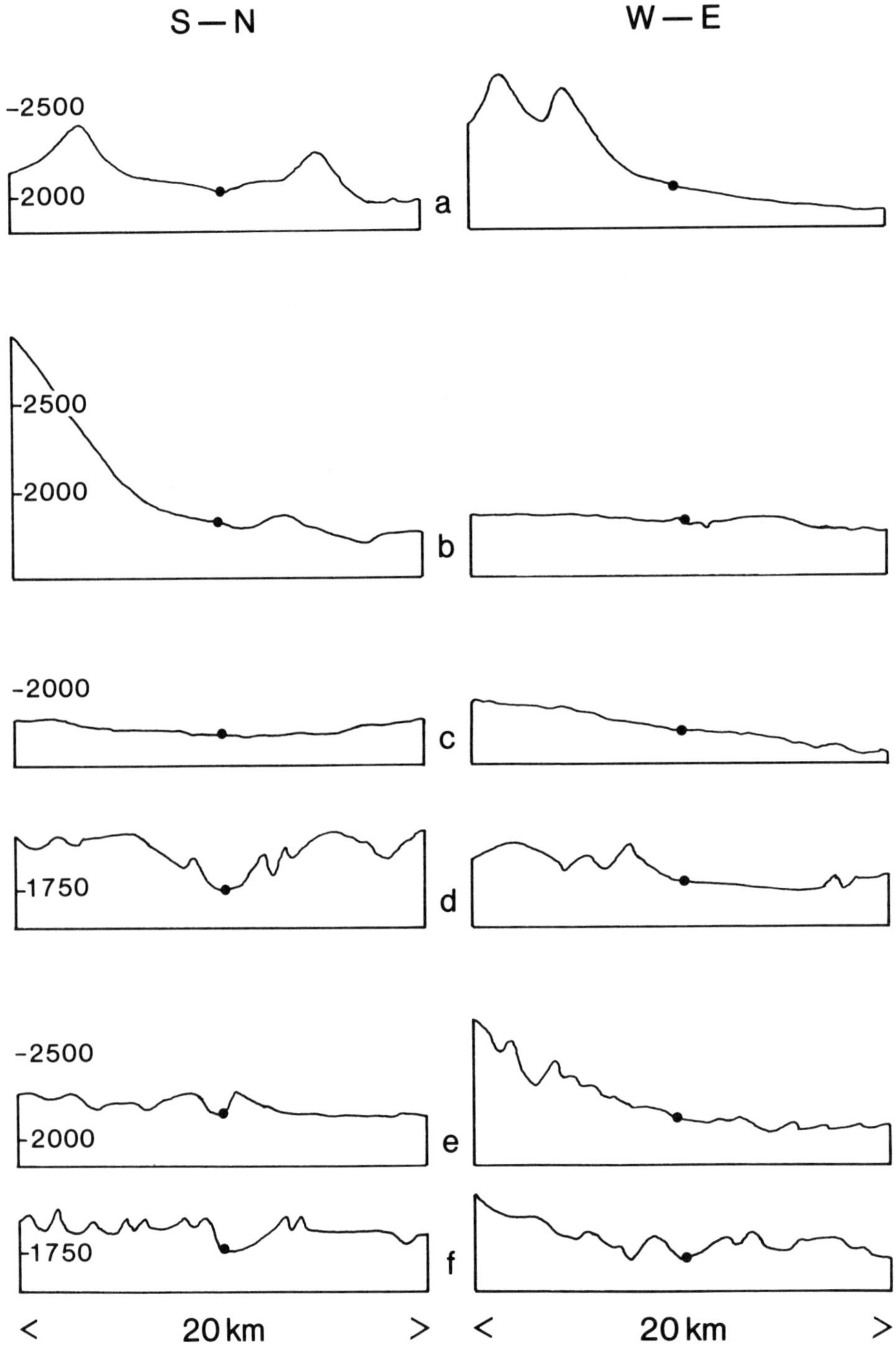

Figure 7. Topographic transects for six Sierra Blanca sites. Note vertical exaggeration. a=Phillips; b=Block Lookout; c=Hiner; d=Bonnell; e=Angus; f=Penasco. Elevations in meters.

was the same as Glencoe Phase people, but more of the meat supply was contributed by antelope; or the increased relative importance of antelope is the result of greater absolute quantities of antelope, such that Lincoln Phase people ate more meat <u>per capita</u> than Glencoe Phase people. If the former situation is correct, and the <u>per capita</u> consumption of meat was the same from one site to another, then the relative frequency of species reflects a variety of hunting patterns directed towards the same end. If the latter is correct, then one may speculate that the importance of agriculture also varied from one area to another, because the amount of time and effort devoted to hunting would vary from site to site.

Unfortunately, it is very difficult to measure the "influx" of bones per year on to a given area of site. One possible method is to compare the rate of bone deposition with the rate of artifact deposition. If one assumes that there is a constant "rain" of artifacts, then variations in the relative influx of bones can be measured. In Table 29 the number of unmodified medium ungulate long-bone ends is compared with the number of artifacts formed of medium ungulate long-bone ends.

TABLE 29

RELATIONSHIP BETWEEN MEDIUM UNGULATE LONG BONES USED AS ARTIFACTS AND PERCENTAGE OF MEDIUM UNGULATES IN SITE ASSEMBLAGES

	Number of Unmodified Long-Bone Ends	Number of Long-Bone Ends Used as Artifacts	% Long-Bone Ends Used as Artifacts	% Medium Ungulates in Lagomorph/Medium Ungulate/Large Ungulate Assemblage
Bonnell	135	26	16.1	25.9
Penasco	27	3	10.0	49.7
Phillips	260	2	0.8	79.2
Block	44	1	2.2	66.0
Hiner	21	1	4.5	83.5

There is considerable variation from one assemblage to another. Figure 8 plots the percentage of such artifacts in the medium ungulate assemblage against the percentage of medium ungulates in the lagomorph/medium ungulate/large ungulate unmodified assemblage. There is an inverse relationship between the two values. At sites with low percentages of medium ungulate bone a relatively high percentage of that bone was utilized as artifacts. If we assume that the need for bone artifacts was constant from site to site, then we may postulate that there was an absolutely greater influx of medium ungulate bone at sites where the medium ungulates form a high proportion of the total assemblage of unworked bone.

On the basis of the above argument, the Lincoln Phase villages were consuming greater quantities of meat, as well as hunting animals in different proportions, when compared to Glencoe Phase villages to the south. This increase is primarily due to the increased use of antelope. Antelope were probably hunted communally in this area, perhaps in contrast to the situation in the Glencoe area where deer may have been hunted individually. The unfortunately small samples of medium ungulate mandibles from Bonnell and Phillips seem to provide evidence for different hunting practices, with greater quantities of immature animals being taken at Phillips. One would expect communal hunting of antelope to result in a substantial proportion of young animals reaching the village sites (e.g., Nimmo 1971).

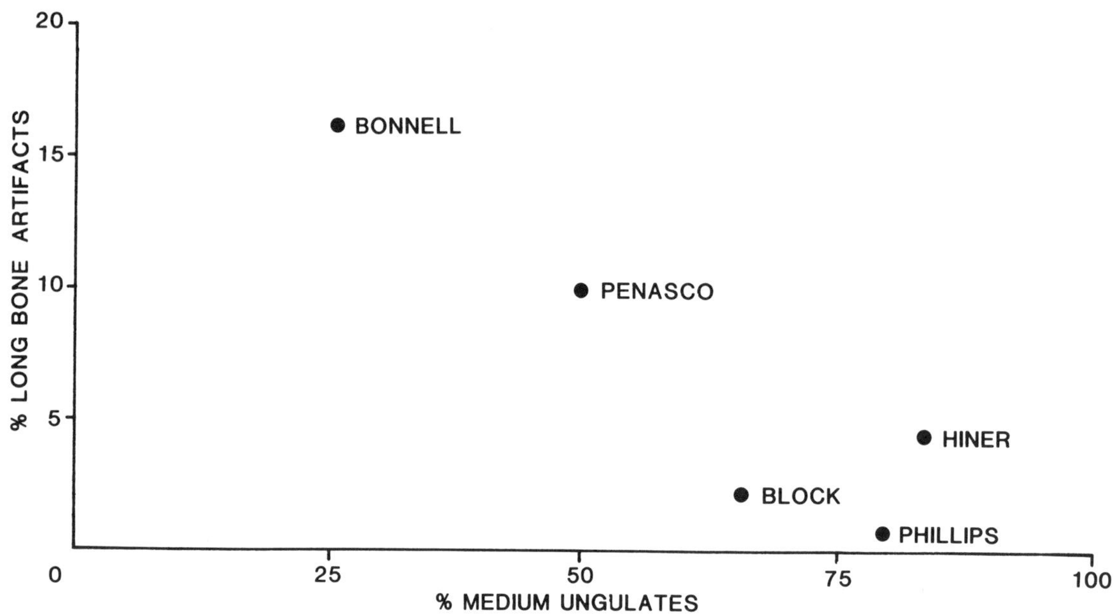

Figure 8. Percentage of medium ungulates (deer, antelope, and medium ungulate) in five Sierra Blanca sites (see Table 29) plotted against percentage of medium ungulate long bones converted to artifacts from each of same five assemblages.

4
SUBSISTENCE IN THE SIERRA BLANCA REGION

It would be premature to suggest that we can reconstruct more than a sketch of prehistoric subsistence in the Sierra Blanca region. The majority of faunal assemblages studied are from archaeological sites excavated thirty years ago, and chronological control is often poor. Furthermore, animal remains cannot be considered in isolation from plant foods, yet our knowledge of agriculture in the region is substantially less complete than our knowledge of faunal remains. Research being conducted now by a number of investigators will help define subsistence strategies more precisely, but some initial formulations can be made on the basis of this study.

The animal component of human subsistence in the Sierra Blanca region was probably directed towards acquisition of protein. Speth and Spielmann (1983) have discussed the importance of animal fat in human diets. I suspect that this was not a major issue in the Sierra Blanca, where agriculture provided a supply of carbohydrates in the form of corn. The low frequency of lower limb bones of deer and antelope also suggests a lack of concern with high-fat areas of the skeleton. Furthermore, many of the species represented on the sites are generally low in fat. This includes antelope and the lagomorphs (Speth and Spielmann 1983:Table 2). In addition to protein, one should not forget that animals would have supplied a number of useful products such as hide and bone.

Considering the faunal assemblages within the context of local environmental conditions, it would appear that there is some correlation between the relative frequency of species in an assemblage and the type of environment around the site. The most notable differences between assemblages lie in the frequency of the medium-sized ungulates in each assemblage, and also in the relative frequency of the two medium-sized ungulate species, deer and antelope. Sites in or adjacent to extensive grasslands contain assemblages dominated by medium-sized ungulates, with antelope far more important than deer. Sites in dissected environments adjacent to permanent watercourses contain fewer medium-sized ungulates, and the ungulate assemblage is dominated by deer. I have suggested that these differences are primarily due to the species composition within the local environment. Furthermore, antelope were hunted by communal means (particularly during the spring), and this results in large accumulations of antelope bones.

It has been noted that differences in local environments have not affected the relative frequencies of the lagomorphs, even though one would expect jackrabbits to be common in the grassland areas. This may be the result of different hunting strategies employed for small and large mammals. If small mammals were collected locally around habitation sites and fields, then cottontails might be expected to turn up more frequently than jackrabbits in most sites. In order for jackrabbits to be hunted from sites containing grassland within their catchment areas, trips away from the sites would be necessary. This does not seem to have happened to any extent.

Bison contributed to the diet of the region's inhabitants, but it is difficult to assess their importance. It is unlikely that bison were present in the region prehistorically, and the bones commonly found on archaeological sites suggest long-distance transport of meat. Whether this was through trade or through participation of Sierra Blanca hunters in long-range hunting expeditions cannot be decided by present evidence. If either process was present, one should consider the possibility that quantities of preserved bison meat might also have entered the sites, but that there is no archaeological representation of this because the preserved meat had been deboned. There is some archaeological evidence for contact between the Sierra Blanca region and the most western Plains groups. Spielmann (1983) has reviewed the evidence from areas to the north of this study area. Wiseman (1984) has pointed out that much of the pottery found at the Garnsey Spring Campsite in the Pecos Valley may have been made in the Sierra Blanca region. He has also recorded pottery from the site which originated hundreds of kilometers west and northwest of the site location. Kelley (1966) suggested that Bloom Mound may have been an important trade center between the Plains and Southwest.

If trade in bison meat did take place, there are many commodities available in the Southwest which would have been desirable items for Plains groups (Spielmann 1983). One should not ignore the possibility that subsistence items might have been traded from the Sierra Blanca to the edge of the Plains. In this regard it is worth considering the possibility that agricultural produce might have been traded from some areas of the Sierra Blanca. Speth (1983) has suggested that low carbohydrate supplies during the spring lead horticultural groups in the Pecos Valley to acquire bison fat. The Sierra Blanca faunal assemblages have not demonstrated a pronounced interest in animal-fat processing. Indeed, the strong evidence for communal hunting of antelope (a low-fat species) in the spring might imply that carbohydrates were more than adequate. Clearly, a detailed evaluation of the agricultural potential of the Sierra Blanca region is required before one can pursue this topic in more detail, but the possibility that corn was traded from the Sierra Blanca region should be considered.

One can suggest that the animal component of human diet in the Sierra Blanca region was obtained from a number of different sources. I propose that small mammals, notably lagomorphs, were hunted close to sites. As the relative frequency of different lagomorph species does not vary markedly, it is possible that these animals were not the subject of major hunting endeavors very far from the villages. Taking of deer and antelope was obviously conducted at greater distances from the sites; presumably the greater body weights compensated for increased travel distances and, in the case of communal antelope hunting, for increased organizational time. Finally, an unknown amount of bison meat found its way to the villages through trade or long-range expeditions.

The relationship of hunting to agriculture is likely to have been complex. Scheduling of hunting may have been partially related to the agricultural cycle; agricultural practices may have affected local population densities of small mammals; the nutritional consequences of agriculture may have directed hunting towards specific types of animal. Analysis of agricultural practices in the Sierra Blanca region can be undertaken through paleoethnobotany, through studies of settlement patterns and site location, and through analysis of agricultural features such as water-control systems. Speth and Scott (1983, 1984, 1985) have suggested that there may have been an intensification of agricultural practices in the Sierra Blanca region, leading to an increased emphasis on large mammals. Until better temporal control is available for the region, this hypothesis will remain largely untested. I have suggested (Driver 1984a) that concentration upon locally available species at Bonnell and Penasco indicates intensive agricultural practices, while hunting of antelope at Phillips, Block Lookout, and Hiner is compatible with less intensive agriculture. This too requires testing.

While this study has been able to summarize aspects of the subsistence base of the Sierra Blanca region, it should be clear from the preceding paragraphs that any viable, testable models of subsistence strategies can only be achieved through interdisciplinary approaches. In particular, one needs to be able to evaluate the agricultural basis of the economy, but trade relationships between sites and extra-regionally will also be important.

5
CONCLUSIONS

Throughout the analysis of the six Sierra Blanca assemblages, problems relating to bone recovery methods have occurred, and such problems have constrained the analysis at various points. Furthermore, lack of contextual evidence has also hampered analysis and interpretation. These points were considered at the start of the paper, and a series of guidelines were employed to avoid making errors in analysis as a result of poor sample quality. Nevertheless, some conclusions concerning the zooarchaeology of the Sierra Blanca region can be made.

Relatively little has been determined concerning the past environment of the area, mainly because small rodents were lacking from the assemblages. However, the presence of muskrat at Penasco and Bonnell allows one to conclude that the sites were situated on permanent rivers, as they are today. The only species present in the sites which is not found in the area today is bison. Given the highly skewed distribution of bison elements, it is likely that bison was hunted at a distance from most sites, and does not seem to have been common west of the Pecos.

The mammalian assemblages can be divided into the following groups:

a. consumed animals--deer, antelope, and bison;

b. probably hunted by humans, but not necessarily consumed--mountain lion, bobcat, canids, and bear;

c. probably hunted and consumed--cottontail and jackrabbit;

d. probably not hunted by humans, but frequent on the site--prairie dog and ground squirrel;

e. status uncertain due to small samples--all other species.

Of these groups, only group "d" is likely to be controversial, because the presence of prairie dog could be due to human hunting and consumption in spite of the evidence which suggests that it was not. Again, better excavated samples are required to resolve the question of whether or not considerable quantities of large sciurids were intrusive to sites.

Accepting the groups as given above, one can define three major types of hunted and consumed mammals--lagomorphs, medium-sized ungulates, and large ungulates. Traditionally, the first two groups supplied a major component of animal meat to horticultural Southwestern cultures, and their prominence is confirmed also for the Sierra Blanca region. The presence of bison on the Sierra Blanca sites reflects their proximity to the Plains, and one might speculate that quite a lot of dried bison meat found its way to the Sierra Blanca region in a deboned condition.

Relatively little can be said about hunting strategies for individual species at the Sierra Blanca sites, because little data exists to show at which season the animals were hunted or the age structure of the hunted assemblage. Data from rabbit bones suggest a fairly indiscriminate predation pattern. Antelope specimens from Phillips show a relatively strong emphasis on young animals, and the presence of fetal/neonatal specimens does demonstrate spring hunting, probably by communal methods. In contrast, the Bonnell data suggest hunting of more mature deer and antelope. Analysis of element frequency for rabbits is made difficult by collection methods. Element frequency for medium ungulates shows that most parts of the skeleton were brought back to the villages. However, there is some indication of differential transport of the limb bones of medium-sized ungulates, particularly at the Phillips site. This may be related to the amount of meat surrounding the bones and to the volume of the marrow cavity.

As one would expect, as one moves from detailed consideration of individual species to inter-site comparisons, the value of the "old" assemblages increases, because major pattern changes show up. I have discussed these in detail elsewhere in the text, and have suggested that differences between faunal assemblages of Glencoe and Corona-Lincoln Phase sites are not the result of increased emphasis on the hunting of medium and large mammals through time, but that the assemblages demonstrate a simple dichotomy between two different environmental situations. These differences are at the micro level (Bonnell, Penasco, and Angus are all on permanent streams) and at the macro level (there are environmental differences between the region containing the Glencoe Phase sites and the region containing the Corona-Lincoln Phase sites). This interpretation contrasts with that of Speth and Scott (1983, 1984, 1985) who favor socioeconomic change as the main reason for a change in faunal use. I have discussed their argument in some detail elsewhere, and believe that it rests upon flaws in dating methodology rather than upon flaws in theory. There are certainly ways in which one could test my interpretation and theirs. First, one should attempt to excavate a Glencoe Phase site which lies in a similar environmental position to the excavated sites of the Corona-Lincoln Phase. Secondly, one could attempt to study change through time in faunal remains on the basis of large samples from carefully excavated deposits of known age. Contextual problems are likely to be a severe restraint in any refinement of a sequence of faunal assemblages. At present I regard my interpretation as the most parsimonious, but further investigation may reveal temporal trends that I have been unable to detect. However, as I have pointed out elsewhere, documentation of temporal trends by Speth and Scott is dubious, and data from Kelley's six sites cannot be used to support temporal trends. Inclusion of both Angus faunas in my analysis simply demonstrates that the site is more similar to Bonnell and Penasco than to Phillips, Hiner, and Block, a result which could be predicted by its environmental position.

Finally, one may conclude that the analysis of assemblages collected over 30 years ago by techniques which might now seem rather simple is justified provided that one is willing to accept that certain areas of information will be lacking. As I stated at the beginning of this paper, we should attempt to formulate initial research problems by considering previously excavated assemblages, and then attempt to refine our interpretations by carefully directed excavations designed to solve specific problems. Future research in the Sierra Blanca region may demonstrate that the "environmentalist" orientation of my analysis is overly simplistic. Certainly, at one level of analysis, the local environment has affected the structure of faunal assemblages recovered from sites in the region. However, Speth and Scott's suggestion of faunal change at the Angus site requires further investigation on larger assemblages in a variety of environmental settings. It may well be that subsistence change through time will be documented, but only within the context of adaptation to local environments.

Appendix
Assemblage Descriptions

Tables A1 to A100 provide a detailed breakdown of faunal assemblages from six sites by taxon, element, and breakage unit. Element is identified in the left-hand column of each table. Breakage units 1 through 8 are represented in the first eight columns of figures. Breakage units are defined in Table 1 of the main text. Note that some elements do not have eight breakage units, and that the definition of a breakage unit varies from one element to another. For example, element category "cranial" has only four breakage units defined in Table 1, while element category "long bone" has eight. Using the same elements, breakage unit 4 for cranial refers to a skull fragment, while breakage unit 4 for a long bone refers to a proximal unfused epiphysis.

TABLE A1
BONNELL *SYLVILAGUS* BY ELEMENT AND BREAKAGE UNIT

Element	1	2	3	4	5	6	7	8	NISP	NDP	MNI
Cranial	15	16		4					35	46	25
Mandible	17	7		69	13	14	41		161	154	89
Vertebrae	24								24	24	-
Scapula		61	26						87	61	35
Humerus	1	16	22		6	31		10	86	77	22
Radius	10	10	3		7			2	32	40	13
Ulna	5	23	4		3			3	38	40	18
Metacarpus	6								6	12	1
Pelvis	10	106	13		19	2	19		169	154	82
Femur	2	29	50		10	59		15	165	152	42
Tibia	1	34	47		6	28		44	160	117	42
Tarsals	20								20	20	9
Metatarsus	42	8	1		2				53	95	6
Total									1036	992	89

TABLE A2
BONNELL *LEPUS* BY ELEMENT AND BREAKAGE UNIT

Element	1	2	3	4	5	6	7	8	NISP	NDP	MNI
Cranial		9							9	9	5
Mandible	2	3		13	5	1	7		31	28	15
Vertebrae	10								10	10	-
Scapula		19	7						26	19	10
Humerus		2	6		1	14		3	26	23	9
Radius	1	5	10		2	7		9	34	26	9
Ulna		4	11			1		4	20	16	9
Metacarpus	2								2	4	1
Pelvis	4	13			3	1	1		22	21	14
Femur		1	7		2	14		1	23	24	11
Tibia		1	14		1	6		6	28	22	9
Tarsals	6								6	6	1
Metatarsus	7	5			1				13	20	2
Total									250	228	15

TABLE A3
BONNELL *SPERMOPHILUS* BY ELEMENT AND BREAKAGE UNIT

Element	1	2	3	4	5	6	7	8	NISP	NDP	MNI
Cranial		3							3	3	2
Mandible	13			12	3	1	1		30	30	19
Total									33	33	19

TABLE A4

BONNELL *CYNOMYS* BY ELEMENT AND BREAKAGE UNIT

Element	1	2	3	4	5	6	7	8	NISP	NDP	MNI
Cranial	1	17							18	19	9
Mandible	23	1		26	9		4		63	62	34
Total									81	81	34

TABLE A5

BONNELL LARGE SCIURID BY ELEMENT AND BREAKAGE UNIT

Element	1	2	3	4	5	6	7	8	NISP	NDP	MNI
Vertebrae	3								3	3	-
Scapula	5	15	4						24	20	15
Humerus	29	4	3		14	11		11	72	90	28
Radius	7	3			1				11	18	6
Ulna	8	9	2		1			6	26	28	11
Pelvis	1	39	4		5	2	2		53	47	24
Femur	23	20	11		10	1		8	73	88	30
Tibia	21	22	4		14	1		5	67	83	31
Total									329	377	31

TABLE A6

BONNELL *THOMOMYS* BY ELEMENT AND BREAKAGE UNIT

Element	1	2	3	4	5	6	7	8	NISP	NDP	MNI
Cranial	1	10		4					15	12	6
Mandible	53								53	53	31
Humerus	1								1	2	1
Pelvis	5	3							8	8	3
Femur	3								3	6	3
Tibia	2								2	4	2
Total									82	85	31

TABLE A7

BONNELL *PEROMYSCUS* BY ELEMENT AND BREAKAGE UNIT

Element	1	2	3	4	5	6	7	8	NISP	NDP	MNI
Mandible	2								2	2	1
Total									2	2	1

TABLE A8
BONNELL NEOTOMA BY ELEMENT AND BREAKAGE UNIT

Element	1	2	3	4	5	6	7	8	NISP	NDP	MNI
Mandible	5			4					9	9	5
Total									9	9	5

TABLE A9
BONNELL ONDATRA ZIBETHICUS BY ELEMENT AND BREAKAGE UNIT

Element	1	2	3	4	5	6	7	8	NISP	NDP	MNI
Mandible	3			1	2				6	6	4
Scapula		1	1						2	1	1
Humerus	2								2	4	2
Radius	1								1	2	1
Ulna		1						1	2	1	1
Pelvis					1	1			2	1	1
Femur	1								1	2	1
Tibia			1						1	1	1
Total									17	18	4

TABLE A10
BONNELL MICROTUS BY ELEMENT AND BREAKAGE UNIT

Element	1	2	3	4	5	6	7	8	NISP	NDP	MNI
Mandible	1			1					2	2	1
Total									2	2	1

TABLE A11
BONNELL ERETHIZON DORSATUM BY ELEMENT AND BREAKAGE UNIT

Element	1	2	3	4	5	6	7	8	NISP	NDP	MNI
Mandible						1			1	1	1
Total									1	1	1

TABLE A12
BONNELL SMALL RODENT BY ELEMENT AND BREAKAGE UNIT

Element	1	2	3	4	5	6	7	8	NISP	NDP	MNI
Cranial		1							1	1	-
Vertebrae	50								50	50	-
Rib	41								41	41	-
Scapula			1						1	-	-
Humerus	2								2	4	-
Radius	6								6	12	-
Pelvis	9								9	9	-
Femur	7	2							9	16	-
Tibia	8								8	16	-
Metapodial	10								10	20	-
Total									137	169	-

TABLE A13
BONNELL *CANIS* BY ELEMENT AND BREAKAGE UNIT

Element	1	2	3	4	5	6	7	8	NISP	NDP	MNI
Cranial		1		1					2	1	1
Mandible		1	2						3	1	2
Rib		1							1	1	1
Humerus						2			2	2	2
Radius	1		2					2	5	4	2
Ulna	1		1					1	3	3	2
Metacarpus	2								2	4	1
Femur		1							1	1	1
Tibia						1			1	1	1
Fibula					1	1			2	2	1
Tarsals	1								1	1	1
Metatarsus					1				1	1	1
1 Phal.	1								1	2	1
Total									25	24	2

TABLE A14
BONNELL *UROCYON CINEREOARGENTEUS* BY ELEMENT AND BREAKAGE UNIT

Element	1	2	3	4	5	6	7	8	NISP	NDP	MNI
Cranial		1		1					2	1	1
Mandible	1								1	1	1
Total									3	2	1

TABLE A15
BONNELL FOX BY ELEMENT AND BREAKAGE UNIT

Element	1	2	3	4	5	6	7	8	NISP	NDP	MNI
Cranial				1					1	1	1
Humerus			2			1			3	3	2
Radius			1			1			2	2	1
Ulna		1						1	2	1	1
Pelvis						1	1		2	1	1
Femur			2			1			3	3	1
Tibia			1			1			2	2	1
Total									15	13	2

TABLE A16
BONNELL *URSUS* BY ELEMENT AND BREAKAGE UNIT

Element	1	2	3	4	5	6	7	8	NISP	NDP	MNI
Tooth								1	1	-	1
Total									1	-	1

TABLE A17
BONNELL *MUSTELA FRENATA* BY ELEMENT AND BREAKAGE UNIT

Element	1	2	3	4	5	6	7	8	NISP	NDP	MNI
Mandible	1								1	1	1
Total									1	1	1

TABLE A18
BONNELL *MEPHITIS MEPHITIS* BY ELEMENT AND BREAKAGE UNIT

Element	1	2	3	4	5	6	7	8	NISP	NDP	MNI
Cranial		1							1	1	1
Mandible	2								2	2	2
Scapula		1							1	1	1
Ulna		2							2	2	2
Femur	1	1	1						3	4	2
Total									9	10	2

TABLE A19
BONNELL *FELIS CONCOLOR* BY ELEMENT AND BREAKAGE UNIT

Element	1	2	3	4	5	6	7	8	NISP	NDP	MNI
Metacarpus	2								2	4	1
1 Phal.	1	1							2	3	1
Total									4	7	1

TABLE A20
BONNELL *LYNX RUFUS* BY ELEMENT AND BREAKAGE UNIT

Element	1	2	3	4	5	6	7	8	NISP	NDP	MNI
Mandible					1				1	1	1
Pelvis	1								1	1	1
Femur			1						1	1	1
Total									3	3	1

TABLE A21
BONNELL *ODOCOILEUS* BY ELEMENT AND BREAKAGE UNIT

Element	1	2	3	4	5	6	7	8	NISP	NDP	MNI
Antler			16						16	-	1
Cranial		1	6	3					10	7	4
Mandible	2	1			2	1	1		7	6	4
Scapula		3							3	3	2
Humerus			2		1	4			7	7	3
Radius		1	2		1	5			9	9	4
Ulna			2						2	2	1
Carpals	9								9	9	2
Metacarpus	1		4		1	1		1	8	8	3
Pelvis		1	3	1		1			6	2	2
Femur			2			2		1	5	4	2
Patella	2								2	2	1
Tibia		1	4	1		4			10	10	3
Tarsals	16	2							18	16	4
Metatarsus			3				1		4	4	3
1 Phal.	14			4					18	32	3
2 Phal.	11	1							12	23	2
3 Phal.	6								6	6	1
Total									152	150	4

TABLE A22
BONNELL *ANTILOCAPRA AMERICANA* BY ELEMENT AND BREAKAGE UNIT

Element	1	2	3	4	5	6	7	8	NISP	NDP	MNI
Horn core		1	2						3	1	1
Cranial			2	3					5	2	1
Mandible			1	4					5	4	2
Scapula	1	1							2	2	1
Humerus			1			3			4	4	3
Radius			3		2	1			6	6	3
Ulna			2						2	2	1
Metacarpus			2			1			3	3	1
Pelvis		2	1			2			5	2	2
Femur			1			2			3	3	2
Tibia			3	2	1	3			9	9	4
Tarsals	7	2							9	7	3
Metatarsus	1		2			3	1		7	8	3
1 Phal.	7								7	14	1
2 Phal.	6	1							7	13	2
3 Phal.	5								5	5	1
Total									82	85	4

TABLE A23
BONNELL MEDIUM UNGULATE BY ELEMENT AND BREAKAGE UNIT

Element	1	2	3	4	5	6	7	8	NISP	NDP	MNI
Cranial			10	76					86	10	-
Mandible		6	4		4		1	14	29	5	-
Cervical		9	7	4					20	11	-
Thoracic	4	16	6	1					27	11	-
Lumbar		22	5	2					29	7	-
Sacrum		9							9	-	-
Caudal	4		1						5	5	-
Vertebrae		11	3		10				24	3	-
Rib		15	33	302	26				376	48	-
Scapula		8	23						31	8	-
Humerus	1		2	2		7		17	29	13	-
Radius			1					20	21	1	-
Ulna			4	1		2		13	20	7	-
Metacarpus			5			3		13	21	8	-
Pelvis			3	4		7		22	36	4	-
Femur		1	3			7	1	27	39	12	-
Tibia			6	3				36	45	9	-
Metatarsus	1		2		1		1	28	33	6	-
Metapodial					2	10	8	15	35	20	-
1 Phal.				5	1				6	5	-
2 Phal.	1	1							2	3	-
Total									923	196	-

TABLE A24
BONNELL BISON BY ELEMENT AND BREAKAGE UNIT

Element	1	2	3	4	5	6	7	8	NISP	NDP	MNI
Cervical		2							2	-	1
Thoracic		16							16	-	1
Lumbar		1							1	-	1
Rib		8	5						13	13	2
Humerus			1					4	5	1	1
Radius			1						1	1	1
Femur			1					4	5	1	1
Tibia								4	4	-	1
Total									47	16	2

TABLE A25
BONNELL LARGE UNGULATE BY ELEMENT AND BREAKAGE UNIT

Element	1	2	3	4	5	6	7	8	NISP	NDP	MNI
Vertebrae		1			1				2	-	-
Rib				281	7				288	-	-
Total									290	-	-

TABLE A26
BONNELL SMALL MAMMAL BY ELEMENT AND BREAKAGE UNIT

Element	1	2	3	4	5	6	7	8	NISP	NDP	MNI
Cranial				80					80	-	-
Axial								35	35	-	-
Long bone								277	277	-	-
Phalanges	9								9	18	-
Total									401	18	-

TABLE A27
BONNELL MEDIUM MAMMAL BY ELEMENT AND BREAKAGE UNIT

Element	1	2	3	4	5	6	7	8	NISP	NDP	MNI
Cranial				142					142	-	-
Axial								955	955	-	-
Long bone								559	559	-	-
Total									1656	-	-

TABLE A28
BONNELL LARGE MAMMAL BY ELEMENT AND BREAKAGE UNIT

Element	1	2	3	4	5	6	7	8	NISP	NDP	MNI
Axial								128	128	-	-
Long bone								25	25	-	-
Total									153	-	-

TABLE A29
BONNELL UNIDENTIFIED BY ELEMENT AND BREAKAGE UNIT

Element	1	2	3	4	5	6	7	8	NISP	NDP	MNI
Unidentified								82	82	-	-
Total									82	-	-

TABLE A30
PENASCO *SYLVILAGUS* BY ELEMENT AND BREAKAGE UNIT

Element	1	2	3	4	5	6	7	8	NISP	NDP	MNI
Cranial			1	1					2	1	1
Mandible		1		2			2		5	4	2
Sacrum	1								1	1	1
Scapula		3	1						4	3	2
Humerus			1					1	2	1	1
Radius			1		1	1			3	3	2
Ulna		1	2						3	3	2
Pelvis	1	11			1		1		14	14	9
Femur		1	3		2				6	6	3
Tibia		1	3		1	1			6	6	3
Metatarsus	2								2	4	1
Total									48	46	9

TABLE A31
PENASCO *LEPUS* BY ELEMENT AND BREAKAGE UNIT

Element	1	2	3	4	5	6	7	8	NISP	NDP	MNI
Mandible			4	2		1			7	3	2
Scapula		5							5	5	3
Humerus		1	3			6			10	10	4
Radius		1			1			1	3	2	1
Ulna		1	1					2	4	2	1
Pelvis		5		1	1	1			8	7	5
Femur		1	2		1	6			10	10	5
Tibia			2			2		1	5	4	2
Metatarsus	1	2						1	4	4	1
Total									56	47	5

TABLE A32
PENASCO *CYNOMYS* BY ELEMENT AND BREAKAGE UNIT

Element	1	2	3	4	5	6	7	8	NISP	NDP	MNI
Cranial			1						1	1	1
Mandible	4		1	2					7	6	3
Total									8	7	3

TABLE A33
PENASCO LARGE SCIURID BY ELEMENT AND BREAKAGE UNIT

Element	1	2	3	4	5	6	7	8	NISP	NDP	MNI
Humerus		2							2	2	2
Radius	1	1			1				3	4	1
Ulna		1						1	2	1	1
Pelvis				1					1	1	1
Tibia								1	1	-	1
Total									9	8	-

TABLE A34
PENASCO *THOMOMYS* BY ELEMENT AND BREAKAGE UNIT

Element	1	2	3	4	5	6	7	8	NISP	NDP	MNI
Mandible	4								4	4	2
Total									4	4	2

TABLE A35
PENASCO *ONDATRA ZIBETHICUS* BY ELEMENT AND BREAKAGE UNIT

Element	1	2	3	4	5	6	7	8	NISP	NDP	MNI
Cranial				1					1	-	1
Mandible	2						4		6	6	4
Sacrum	1								1	1	1
Scapula		1							1	1	1
Humerus		1							1	1	1
Pelvis			1						1	-	1
Femur					1			1	2	1	1
Tibia	1								1	2	1
Total									14	12	4

TABLE A36
PENASCO SMALL RODENT BY ELEMENT AND BREAKAGE UNIT

Element	1	2	3	4	5	6	7	8	NISP	NDP	MNI
Cranial				6					6	-	-
Vertebrae	2								2	2	-
Rib		2		1					3	2	-
Radius	1								1	2	-
Ulna								1	1	-	-
1 Phal.	1								1	2	-
Total									14	8	-

TABLE A37
PENASCO *MEPHITIS MEPHITIS* BY ELEMENT AND BREAKAGE UNIT

Element	1	2	3	4	5	6	7	8	NISP	NDP	MNI
Pelvis		1							1	1	1
Femur		1							1	1	1
Total									2	2	1

TABLE A38
PENASCO *LYNX* BY ELEMENT AND BREAKAGE UNIT

Element	1	2	3	4	5	6	7	8	NISP	NDP	MNI
Radius		1							1	1	1
Total									1	1	1

TABLE A39
PENASCO ODOCOILEUS BY ELEMENT AND BREAKAGE UNIT

Element	1	2	3	4	5	6	7	8	NISP	NDP	MNI
Antler		1	4						5	1	1
Cranial		2							2	2	2
Scapula		2							2	2	1
Humerus						1			1	1	1
Radius		1	4						5	5	3
Ulna								1	1	-	1
Metacarpus	1					1			2	3	2
Pelvis		3							3	-	1
Femur		1	1		3	3			8	8	3
Patella	1								1	1	1
Tibia			2			1			3	3	1
Tarsals	7	1							8	7	3
Metatarsus			1						1	1	1
1 Phal.	4								4	8	2
2 Phal.	5								5	10	1
3 Phal.	5								5	5	1
Total									56	57	3

TABLE A40
PENASCO ANTILOCAPRA AMERICANA BY ELEMENT AND BREAKAGE UNIT

Element	1	2	3	4	5	6	7	8	NISP	NDP	MNI
Mandible				1					1	1	1
Humerus		2							2	2	2
Pelvis					1				1	1	1
Femur			1						1	1	1
Tibia			1						1	1	1
1 Phal.	1								1	2	1
2 Phal.	1								1	2	1
3 Phal.	1								1	1	1
Total									9	11	2

TABLE A41
PENASCO MEDIUM UNGULATE BY ELEMENT AND BREAKAGE UNIT

Element	1	2	3	4	5	6	7	8	NISP	NDP	MNI
Cranial				3					3	-	-
Mandible			2		2				4	2	-
Cervical	2	1							3	2	-
Thoracic	1	1	3						5	4	-
Rib		1	2	24					27	3	-
Sternum		1							1	-	-
Scapula			5						5	-	-
Humerus				1				3	4	1	-
Radius								2	2	-	-
Pelvis			1			3			4	-	-
Femur						1		6	7	1	-
Tibia			1			2		4	7	3	-
Metapodial		1	6			1		11	19	8	-
Total									91	24	-

TABLE A42
PENASCO LARGE UNGULATE BY ELEMENT AND BREAKAGE UNIT

Element	1	2	3	4	5	6	7	8	NISP	NDP	MNI
Rib				2					2	-	-
Total									2	-	-

TABLE A43
PENASCO SMALL MAMMAL BY ELEMENT AND BREAKAGE UNIT

Element	1	2	3	4	5	6	7	8	NISP	NDP	MNI
Long bone								25	25	-	-
Total									25	-	-

TABLE A44
PENASCO MEDIUM MAMMAL BY ELEMENT AND BREAKAGE UNIT

Element	1	2	3	4	5	6	7	8	NISP	NDP	MNI
Axial								16	16	-	-
Long bone								93	93	-	-
Total									109	-	-

TABLE A45
PENASCO LARGE MAMMAL BY ELEMENT AND BREAKAGE UNIT

Element	1	2	3	4	5	6	7	8	NISP	NDP	MNI
Axial								1	1	-	-
Long bone								1	1	-	-
Total									2	-	-

TABLE A46
PHILLIPS *SYLVILAGUS* BY ELEMENT AND BREAKAGE UNIT

Element	1	2	3	4	5	6	7	8	NISP	NDP	MNI
Cranial		8							8	8	5
Mandible	1	1		9	7		4		22	22	12
Vertebrae	2								2	2	1
Scapula		9	2						11	9	6
Humerus		4			1				5	5	2
Radius	2	1				1			4	6	2
Ulna	1	2	1		1			1	6	6	3
Pelvis	1	18		2		1	3		25	24	12
Femur	2	10	8		5	7		3	35	34	11
Tibia	1	21	8			4		4	38	35	18
Tarsals	1								1	1	1
Metatarsus	1								1	2	1
Total									158	154	18

TABLE A47
PHILLIPS *LEPUS* BY ELEMENT AND BREAKAGE UNIT

Element	1	2	3	4	5	6	7	8	NISP	NDP	MNI
Mandible				1	1	1			3	3	2
Vertebrae	1	1		1					3	3	1
Rib		1							1	1	1
Scapula		3	1						4	3	3
Humerus	1	1	1			1			4	5	2
Radius	1	1	3						5	6	4
Ulna		3	2						5	5	4
Metacarpus	1								1	2	1
Pelvis		3							3	3	2
Femur			1			3	1		5	5	3
Tibia	1	1	1		1	3		2	9	8	3
Tarsals	2								2	2	1
Metatarsus	3	1	1			1			6	9	1
Total									51	55	4

TABLE A48
PHILLIPS *CYNOMYS* BY ELEMENT AND BREAKAGE UNIT

Element	1	2	3	4	5	6	7	8	NISP	NDP	MNI
Cranial		4							4	4	4
Mandible	10	2		1		1	3		17	15	11
Total									21	19	11

TABLE A49
PHILLIPS LARGE SCIURID BY ELEMENT AND BREAKAGE UNIT

Element	1	2	3	4	5	6	7	8	NISP	NDP	MNI
Vertebrae	5		2						7	7	2
Scapula		3							3	3	3
Humerus	9	2	2		3	1		1	18	26	9
Radius	1	2							3	4	2
Ulna	2	1							3	5	2
Pelvis	1	8	1		1				11	10	7
Femur	10	3	1		2	1			17	27	9
Tibia	3	6						1	10	12	6
Total									72	94	9

TABLE A50
PHILLIPS *THOMOMYS* BY ELEMENT AND BREAKAGE UNIT

Element	1	2	3	4	5	6	7	8	NISP	NDP	MNI
Cranial				2					2	-	1
Mandible	1		1				1		3	2	2
Total									5	2	2

TABLE A51
PHILLIPS *CANIS* BY ELEMENT AND BREAKAGE UNIT

Element	1	2	3	4	5	6	7	8	NISP	NDP	MNI
Rib		1							1	1	1
Metacarpus	2								2	4	1
Metatarsus	2	2							4	6	1
Total									7	11	1

TABLE A52
PHILLIPS *VULPES MACROTIS* BY ELEMENT AND BREAKAGE UNIT

Element	1	2	3	4	5	6	7	8	NISP	NDP	MNI
Scapula	1								1	1	1
Total									1	1	1

TABLE A53
PHILLIPS *TAXIDEA TAXUS* BY ELEMENT AND BREAKAGE UNIT

Element	1	2	3	4	5	6	7	8	NISP	NDP	MNI
Pelvis	2								2	2	1
Total									2	2	1

TABLE A54
PHILLIPS *FELIS CONCOLOR* BY ELEMENT AND BREAKAGE UNIT

Element	1	2	3	4	5	6	7	8	NISP	NDP	MNI
1 Phal.	1								1	2	1
Total									1	2	1

TABLE A55
PHILLIPS *LYNX* BY ELEMENT AND BREAKAGE UNIT

Element	1	2	3	4	5	6	7	8	NISP	NDP	MNI
Radius			1						1	1	1
Pelvis			1						1	-	1
Matatarsus	1								1	2	1
Total									3	3	1

TABLE A56

PHILLIPS <u>ODOCOILEUS</u> BY ELEMENT AND BREAKAGE UNIT

Element	1	2	3	4	5	6	7	8	NISP	NDP	MNI
Antler			8						8	-	1
Cranial			3						3	3	3
Mandible					1	1			2	2	2
Scapula		5	2						7	5	3
Humerus			3			4			7	7	3
Radius						1			1	1	1
Ulna			3						3	3	2
Carpals	1								1	1	1
Metacarpus			1			1			2	2	1
Pelvis		1	2		2	5	1		11	4	2
Femur			5			2	5		12	12	5
Tibia			3	4		4			11	11	5
Tarsals	6	1							7	6	2
Metatarsus			2		1	1			4	4	2
1 Phal.	10	1		1					12	22	3
2 Phal.	5								5	10	1
3 Phal.	4								4	4	1
Total									100	97	5

TABLE A57

PHILLIPS <u>ANTILOCAPRA</u> <u>AMERICANA</u> BY ELEMENT AND BREAKAGE UNIT

Element	1	2	3	4	5	6	7	8	NISP	NDP	MNI
Cranial			6	1					7	6	5
Mandible	3	1	1		6	1	1		13	11	7
Scapula	2	9	2						13	11	6
Humerus			6			17			23	23	12
Radius		2	10		2	5			19	19	10
Ulna			9					1	10	9	5
Carpals	9								9	9	2
Metacarpus		4	2		1	3			10	10	5
Pelvis		1	5	3		12			21	4	2
Femur			11			3	4		18	18	7
Tibia			11	1		8	1		21	21	7
Tarsals	41								41	36	5
Metatarsus	1	1	8		1	4			15	16	6
1 Phal.	53			3	1				57	109	7
2 Phal.	34			1					35	69	5
3 Phal.	20	1							21	21	3
Total									333	392	12

TABLE A58

PHILLIPS MEDIUM UNGULATE BY ELEMENT AND BREAKAGE UNIT

Element	1	2	3	4	5	6	7	8	NISP	NDP	MNI
Cranial			5	115					120	5	-
Hyoid	3								3	-	-
Mandible		1	4			4			9	4	-
Cervical	21	9	7	4					41	32	-
Thoracic	30	35	5						70	35	-
Lumbar	24	17	9	1					51	34	-
Sacrum		6	9						15	9	-
Caudal	3								3	3	-
Vertebrae		5	25		15	15			60	-	-
Rib		67	38	251	25				381	105	-
Sternum	2	9							11	-	-
Scapula	1	8	39						48	9	-
Humerus	2		4	3		7		19	35	18	-
Radius	2	1	6		1	4		7	21	16	-
Ulna			2				1	11	14	3	-
Metacarpus			3			3		6	12	6	-
Pelvis			11			4			15	-	-
Femur	1		8	5		9	3	25	51	27	-
Patella	3								3	3	-
Tibia			14	5	1	4		23	47	24	-
Tarsals	4	6							10	4	-
Metatarsus			1			4		16	21	5	-
Metapodial			1		1	9	20	25	56	31	-
3 Phal.	1	1							2	1	-
Total									1099	374	-

TABLE A59

PHILLIPS BISON BY ELEMENT AND BREAKAGE UNIT

Element	1	2	3	4	5	6	7	8	NISP	NDP	MNI
Mandible							1		1	1	1
Cervical		3		2					5	2	1
Thoracic		4	2						6	2	1
Lumbar		3							3	-	1
Rib		7	4						11	11	1
Metacarpus			1						1	1	1
Femur								1	1	-	1
Tibia								4	4	-	1
Total									32	17	1

TABLE A60
PHILLIPS LARGE UNGULATE BY ELEMENT AND BREAKAGE UNIT

Element	1	2	3	4	5	6	7	8	NISP	NDP	MNI
Rib				132	12				144	-	-
Total									144	-	-

TABLE A61
PHILLIPS SMALL MAMMAL BY ELEMENT AND BREAKAGE UNIT

Element	1	2	3	4	5	6	7	8	NISP	NDP	MNI
Cranial				14					14	-	-
Rib				1					1	-	-
Long bone								20	20	-	-
Total									35	-	-

TABLE A62
PHILLIPS MEDIUM MAMMAL BY ELEMENT AND BREAKAGE UNIT

Element	1	2	3	4	5	6	7	8	NISP	NDP	MNI
Long bone								504	504	-	-
Axial								291	291	-	-
Total									795	-	-

TABLE A63
PHILLIPS LARGE MAMMAL BY ELEMENT AND BREAKAGE UNIT

Element	1	2	3	4	5	6	7	8	NISP	NDP	MNI
Axial								19	19	-	-
Long bone								11	11	-	-
Total									30	-	-

TABLE A64

BLOCK LOOKOUT SYLVILAGUS BY ELEMENT AND BREAKAGE UNIT

Element	1	2	3	4	5	6	7	8	NISP	NDP	MNI
Cranial		1							1	1	1
Mandible							2		2	2	1
Humerus						1			1	1	1
Radius	1								1	2	1
Metacarpus	1								1	2	1
Pelvis	1	1							2	2	1
Femur		2			3			1	6	5	2
Tibia	1	6	1					2	10	9	5
Metatarsus	1								1	2	1
Total									25	26	5

TABLE A65

BLOCK LOOKOUT LEPUS BY ELEMENT AND BREAKAGE UNIT

Element	1	2	3	4	5	6	7	8	NISP	NDP	MNI
Mandible			1						1	-	1
Humerus			1			1			2	2	1
Ulna			2						2	2	2
Pelvis		1	1						2	1	1
Femur	1								1	2	1
Tibia								1	1	-	1
Total									9	7	2

TABLE A66

BLOCK LOOKOUT LARGE SCIURID BY ELEMENT AND BREAKAGE UNIT

Element	1	2	3	4	5	6	7	8	NISP	NDP	MNI
Mandible	1								1	1	1
Ulna	1								1	2	1
Total									2	3	1

TABLE A67

BLOCK LOOKOUT CANIS BY ELEMENT AND BREAKAGE UNIT

Element	1	2	3	4	5	6	7	8	NISP	NDP	MNI
Cranial				1					1	-	1
Tibia						1			1	1	1
Total									2	1	1

TABLE A68
BLOCK LOOKOUT LYNX BY ELEMENT AND BREAKAGE UNIT

Element	1	2	3	4	5	6	7	8	NISP	NDP	MNI
Metatarsus	1								1	2	1
Tarsals	1								1	1	1
Total									2	3	1

TABLE A69
BLOCK LOOKOUT NEOTOMA BY ELEMENT AND BREAKAGE UNIT

Element	1	2	3	4	5	6	7	8	NISP	NDP	MNI
Mandible	1								1	1	1
Total									1	1	1

TABLE A70
BLOCK LOOKOUT ODOCOILEUS BY ELEMENT AND BREAKAGE UNIT

Element	1	2	3	4	5	6	7	8	NISP	NDP	MNI
Antler			1						1	-	1
Humerus		1			1	1			3	3	2
Radius			1						1	1	1
Ulna								1	1	-	1
Metacarpus	2*					1			3	1	1
Pelvis			1	1	1	1			4	2	1
Femur			1						1	1	1
Tibia						1			1	1	1
Tarsals	1								1	1	1
1 Phal.	1								1	2	1
3 Phal.	1								1	1	1
Total									18	13	2

*Metacarpus II/V (not included in NDP figures)

TABLE A71

BLOCK LOOKOUT <u>ANTILOCAPRA</u> <u>AMERICANA</u> BY ELEMENT AND BREAKAGE UNIT

<u>Element</u>	1	2	3	4	5	6	7	8	NISP	NDP	MNI
Horn core		3	1						4	3	2
Cranial		5							5	5	3
Mandible						1	1		2	2	2
Scapula	2	2							4	4	3
Humerus			4			6			10	10	4
Radius			3			2			5	5	2
Ulna			2						2	2	1
Carpals	3								3	3	1
Metacarpus			2		1	1			4	4	2
Pelvis		1		1					2	2	1
Femur			1						1	1	1
Tibia						2			2	2	1
Tarsals	1								1	1	1
Metatarsus			2			1	1		4	4	2
1 Phal.	4			1					5	9	1
2 Phal.	3								3	6	1
3 Phal.	3								3	3	1
Total									60	66	4

TABLE A72

BLOCK LOOKOUT MEDIUM UNGULATE BY ELEMENT AND BREAKAGE UNIT

<u>Element</u>	1	2	3	4	5	6	7	8	NISP	NDP	MNI
Cranial				25					25	-	-
Mandible					1				1	1	-
Cervical	1	2		1					4	2	-
Thoracic	4	6	6						16	10	-
Lumbar	2	2	3						7	5	-
Sacrum		1		1					2	1	-
Rib		8	6	61	12				87	14	-
Sternum	3	1							4	-	-
Scapula			16						16	-	-
Humerus		1	1					3	5	2	-
Radius						1		7	8	1	-
Ulna								2	2	-	-
Pelvis			1					2	3	-	-
Femur				1		2		7	10	3	-
Tibia			3		1		1	1	6	5	-
Tarsals		1							1	-	-
Metatarsus								5	5	-	-
Metapodial						5			5	5	-
Total									207	49	-

TABLE A73
BLOCK LOOKOUT BISON BY ELEMENT AND BREAKAGE UNIT

Element	1	2	3	4	5	6	7	8	NISP	NDP	MNI
Humerus			3					6	9	3	2
Ulna	1		1						2	3	2
Femur			4					4	8	4	3
Tibia			1					2	3	1	1
Total									22	11	3

TABLE A74
BLOCK LOOKOUT LARGE UNGULATE BY ELEMENT AND BREAKAGE UNIT

Element	1	2	3	4	5	6	7	8	NISP	NDP	MNI
Cervical			1	1	1				3	2	-
Thoracic	1	2			1				4	1	-
Lumbar		3	1						4	1	-
Rib		10	8	127	13				158	18	-
Total									169	22	-

TABLE A75
BLOCK LOOKOUT SMALL MAMMAL BY ELEMENT AND BREAKAGE UNIT

Element	1	2	3	4	5	6	7	8	NISP	NDP	MNI
Cranial				4					4	-	-
Lumbar	2		1						3	3	-
Long bone								13	13	-	-
Total									20	3	-

TABLE A76
BLOCK LOOKOUT MEDIUM MAMMAL BY ELEMENT AND BREAKAGE UNIT

Element	1	2	3	4	5	6	7	8	NISP	NDP	MNI
Axial								67	67	-	-
Long bone								96	96	-	-
Total									163	-	-

TABLE A77
BLOCK LOOKOUT LARGE MAMMAL BY ELEMENT AND BREAKAGE UNIT

Element	1	2	3	4	5	6	7	8	NISP	NDP	MNI
Axial								41	41	-	-
Long bone								29	29	-	-
Total									70	-	-

TABLE A78
HINER SYLVILAGUS BY ELEMENT AND BREAKAGE UNIT

Element	1	2	3	4	5	6	7	8	NISP	NDP	MNI
Humerus	1				1				2	3	2
Femur	1	1	2			2			6	7	3
Tibia	1								1	2	1
Total									9	12	3

TABLE A79
HINER LEPUS BY ELEMENT AND BREAKAGE UNIT

Element	1	2	3	4	5	6	7	8	NISP	NDP	MNI
Humerus		1							1	1	1
Radius		1	1						2	2	2
Ulna			1						1	1	1
Pelvis			1						1	-	1
Tibia								1	1	-	1
Total									6	4	2

TABLE A80
HINER THOMOMYS BY ELEMENT AND BREAKAGE UNIT

Element	1	2	3	4	5	6	7	8	NISP	NDP	MNI
Mandible				1					1	1	1
Total									1	1	1

TABLE A81
HINER CANIS BY ELEMENT AND BREAKAGE UNIT

Element	1	2	3	4	5	6	7	8	NISP	NDP	MNI
Cranial				1					1	-	1
Scapula	1								1	1	1
Total									2	1	1

TABLE A82
HINER *ODOCOILEUS* BY ELEMENT AND BREAKAGE UNIT

Element	1	2	3	4	5	6	7	8	NISP	NDP	MNI
Carpals	2								2	2	1
Pelvis			1						1	-	1
Metatarsus						1			1	1	1
1 Phal.		1							1	1	1
2 Phal.	1								1	2	1
Total									6	6	1

TABLE A83
HINER *ANTILOCAPRA AMERICANA* BY ELEMENT AND BREAKAGE UNIT

Element	1	2	3	4	5	6	7	8	NISP	NDP	MNI
Mandible			2					1	3	-	1
Scapula		1							1	1	1
Humerus			1						1	1	1
Radius			3			2			5	5	2
Ulna								1	1	-	1
Carpals	1								1	1	1
Metacarpus						2			2	2	2
Pelvis							1		1	1	1
Patella	1								1	1	1
Tibia			1						1	1	1
Tarsals	4	2							6	4	1
Metatarsus			1		1	1	2		5	5	3
Metapodial						1			1	1	-
1 Phal.	4	2		2					8	12	2
2 Phal.	6								6	12	1
3 Phal.	4								4	4	1
Total									47	51	3

TABLE A84
HINER MEDIUM UNGULATE BY ELEMENT AND BREAKAGE UNIT

Element	1	2	3	4	5	6	7	8	NISP	NDP	MNI
Cervical		1		1					2	1	-
Thoracic	1	4	4		1				10	5	-
Lumbar		4	1						5	1	-
Rib		3		50	2				55	3	-
Sternum	1	1							2	-	-
Scapula	1	1	5						7	2	-
Humerus								1	1	-	-
Radius			1					3	4	1	-
Ulna								3	3	-	-
Carpals	1								1	1	-
Metacarpus			1					1	2	1	-
Pelvis						3			3	-	-
Femur			2			1			3	3	-
Tibia						2		1	3	2	-
Metatarsus								3	3	-	-
Metapodial						3	1		4	4	-
Total									108	24	-

TABLE A85
HINER <u>BISON</u> BY ELEMENT AND BREAKAGE UNIT

Element	1	2	3	4	5	6	7	8	NISP	NDP	MNI
Thoracic		1							1	-	1
Scapula			2						2	-	1
Humerus								1	1	-	1
Femur								1	1	-	1
Tibia								1	1	-	1
Total									6	-	1

TABLE A86
HINER LARGE UNGULATE BY ELEMENT AND BREAKAGE UNIT

Element	1	2	3	4	5	6	7	8	NISP	NDP	MNI
Rib				25	2				27	-	-
Total									27	-	-

TABLE A87
HINER SMALL MAMMAL BY ELEMENT AND BREAKAGE UNIT

Element	1	2	3	4	5	6	7	8	NISP	NDP	MNI
Rib				1					1	-	-
Axial								15	15	-	-
Long bone								3	3	-	-
Total									19	-	-

TABLE A88
HINER MEDIUM MAMMAL BY ELEMENT AND BREAKAGE UNIT

Element	1	2	3	4	5	6	7	8	NISP	NDP	MNI
Cranial				11					11	-	-
Axial								1	1	-	-
Long bone								41	41	-	-
Total									53	-	-

TABLE A89
HINER LARGE MAMMAL BY ELEMENT AND BREAKAGE UNIT

Element	1	2	3	4	5	6	7	8	NISP	NDP	MNI
Long bone								5	5	-	-
Total									5	-	-

TABLE A90
BLOOM MOUND SYLVILAGUS BY ELEMENT AND BREAKAGE UNIT

Element	1	2	3	4	5	6	7	8	NISP	NDP	MNI
Radius								1	1	-	1
Pelvis		1			1				2	2	1
Femur		1							1	1	1
Tibia		1			2				3	3	2
Total									7	6	2

TABLE A91
BLOOM MOUND *LEPUS* BY ELEMENT AND BREAKAGE UNIT

Element	1	2	3	4	5	6	7	8	NISP	NDP	MNI
Mandible					1				1	1	1
Radius								1	1	-	1
Tibia						1			1	1	1
Total									3	2	1

TABLE A92
BLOOM MOUND LARGE SCIURID BY ELEMENT AND BREAKAGE UNIT

Element	1	2	3	4	5	6	7	8	NISP	NDP	MNI
Humerus	2								2	4	1
Radius		1							1	1	1
Ulna		1							1	1	1
Tibia					1				1	1	1
Total									5	7	1

TABLE A93
BLOOM MOUND *CANIS* BY ELEMENT AND BREAKAGE UNIT

Element	1	2	3	4	5	6	7	8	NISP	NDP	MNI
Mandible	1								1	1	1
Pelvis						1			1	-	1
Femur			1						1	1	1
Total									3	2	1

TABLE A94
BLOOM MOUND *ODOCOILEUS* BY ELEMENT AND BREAKAGE UNIT

Element	1	2	3	4	5	6	7	8	NISP	NDP	MNI
Antler			6						6	-	1
Total									6	-	1

TABLE A95
BLOOM MOUND *ANTILOCAPRA AMERICANA* BY ELEMENT AND BREAKAGE UNIT

Element	1	2	3	4	5	6	7	8	NISP	NDP	MNI
Metacarpus						1			1	1	1
Tarsals	1								1	1	1
Total									2	2	1

TABLE A96
BLOOM MOUND MEDIUM UNGULATE BY ELEMENT AND BREAKAGE UNIT

Element	1	2	3	4	5	6	7	8	NISP	NDP	MNI
Thoracic		1							1	-	1
Scapula			1						1	-	1
Metapodial						1			1	1	1
Total									3	1	-

TABLE A97
BLOOM MOUND BISON BY ELEMENT AND BREAKAGE UNIT

Element	1	2	3	4	5	6	7	8	NISP	NDP	MNI
Humerus			1		1				2	2	1
Radius	1								1	2	1
Ulna								1	1	-	1
Pelvis								2	2	-	1
Patella	1								1	1	1
Tibia						1		1	2	1	1
Total									9	6	1

TABLE A98
BLOOM MOUND SMALL MAMMAL BY ELEMENT AND BREAKAGE UNIT

Element	1	2	3	4	5	6	7	8	NISP	NDP	MNI
Long bone								2	2	-	-
Total									2	-	-

TABLE A99
BLOOM MOUND MEDIUM MAMMAL BY ELEMENT AND BREAKAGE UNIT

Element	1	2	3	4	5	6	7	8	NISP	NDP	MNI
Axial								20	20	-	-
Long bone								27	27	-	-
Total									47	-	-

TABLE A100
BLOOM MOUND LARGE MAMMAL BY ELEMENT AND BREAKAGE UNIT

Element	1	2	3	4	5	6	7	8	NISP	NDP	MNI
Axial								13	13	-	-
Long bone								4	4	-	-
Total									17	-	-

REFERENCES CITED

Andrews, P., and E. M. Nesbit Evans
1983 Small mammal bone accumulations produced by mammalian carnivores. Paleobiology 9(3):289-307.

Bailey, V.
1931 Mammals of New Mexico. North American Fauna 53. Washington: United States Department of Agriculture.

Bayham, F. E.
1982 A Diachronic Analysis of Prehistoric Animal Exploitation at Ventana Cave. Unpublished Ph.D. dissertation. Tempe: Arizona State University.

Binford, L. R.
1978 Nunamiut Ethnoarchaeology. New York: Academic Press.

1981 Bones: Ancient Men and Modern Myths. New York: Academic Press.

Brain, C. K.
1981 The Hunters or the Hunted? Chicago: University of Chicago Press.

Brumley, J. H.
1973 Quantitative methods in the analysis of butchered faunal remains: A suggested approach. Archaeology in Montana 14(1):1-40.

Bullock, D., and J. Rackham
1982 Epiphyseal fusion and tooth eruption of feral goats from Moffatdale, Dumfries, and Galloway, Scotland. In Ageing and Sexing Animal Bones from Archaeological Sites, edited by B. Wilson, C. Grigson, and S. Payne, pp. 73-80. British Series 109. Oxford: British Archaeological Reports.

Bunn, H. T.
1981 Archaeological evidence for meat-eating by Plio-Pleistocene hominids from Koobi Fora and Olduvai Gorge. Nature 291(5816):574-576.

Callen, E. O.
1967 Analysis of the Tehuacan coprolites. In The Prehistory of the Tehuacan Valley, Vol. 1, Environment and Subsistence, edited by D.S. Byers, pp. 261-289. Austin: University of Texas Press.

1969 Diet as revealed by coprolites. In Science in Archaeology, 2nd edition, edited by D.R. Brothwell and E.S. Higgs, pp. 235-243. London: Thames and Hudson.

Chaplin, R. E.
1971 The Study of Animal Bones from Archaeological Sites. London: Seminar Press.

Cordell, L. S., and A. C. Earls
1984 The Rio Grande Glaze "Sequence" and the Mogollon. In Recent Research in Mogollon Archaeology, edited by S. Upham, F. Plog, D. G. Batcho, and B. E. Kauffman, pp. 90-97. Occasional Paper 10. Las Cruces: University Museum, New Mexico State University.

Davis, W. B.
1960 The Mammals of Texas. Texas Game and Fish Commission Bulletin 41.

Dodson, P., and D. Wexlar
1979 Taphonomic investigations of owl pellets. Paleobiology 5:275-284.

Driesch, Angela von den
1976 A Guide to the Measurement of Animal Bones from Archaeological Sites. Peabody Museum Bulletin 1. Cambridge: Harvard University.

Driver, J. C.
1982 Zooarchaeology in the Sierra Blanca. Paper presented at the Second Mogollon Conference, Las Cruces, New Mexico, October 1982.

1984a Zooarchaeology in the Sierra Blanca. In Recent Research in Mogollon Archaeology, edited by S. Upham, F. Plog, D. G. Batcho, and B. E. Kauffman, pp. 140-155. Occasional Paper 10. Las Cruces: University Museum, New Mexico State University.

1984b Zooarchaeological analysis of raw material selection by a Saxon artisan. Journal of Field Archaeology 11:397-403.

Foley, R.
1977 Space and energy. In Spatial Archaeology, edited by D. L. Clarke, pp. 163-188. London: Academic Press.

Fox, Sir C.
1923 The Archaeology of the Cambridge Region. Cambridge: Cambridge University Press.

Frison, G. C.
1973 The Wardell Buffalo Trap 48SU301: Communal Procurement in the Upper Green River Basin, Wyoming. Anthropological Paper 48. Ann Arbor: University of Michigan Museum of Anthropology.

Gifford, D. P.
1981 Taphonomy and paleoecology: A critical review of archaeology's sister disciplines. Advances in Archaeological Method and Theory 4:365-438.

Gilbert, B. M.
1973 Mammalian Osteo-archaeology: North America. Columbia: Missouri Archaeological Society.

Grayson, D. K.
1978 Reconstructing mammalian communities: A discussion of Shotwell's method of paleoecological analysis. Paleobiology 4:77-81.

1979 On the quantification of vertebrate archaeofaunas. Advances in Archaeological Method and Theory 2:199-237.

Hale, J. R.
1949 Ageing cottontails by bone growth. Journal of Wildlife Management 13:216-225.

Hall, E. R.
1981 The Mammals of North America, Vols. 1 and 2, 2nd edition. New York: John Wiley and Sons.

Halstead, P., I. Hodder, and G. Jones
1978 Behavioural archaeology and refuse patterns: A case study. Norwegian Archaeological Review 11:118-131.

Haynes, G.
1982 Utilization and skeletal disturbances of North American prey carcasses. Arctic 35(2):266-281.

Heller, M.
1976 Interpretation of vertebrate faunal material from LA2112, Lincoln County, New Mexico. In Multi-disciplinary Investigations at the Smokey Bear Ruin (LA2112), Lincoln County, New Mexico, edited by R. N. Wiseman, pp. 48-54. Las Cruces: COAS.

Higgs, E. S., and M. R. Jarman
1975 Palaeoeconomy. In Palaeoeconomy, edited by E. S. Higgs, pp. 1-7. Cambridge: Cambridge University Press.

Higgs, E. S., and C. Vita-Finzi
1970 Prehistoric economies in the Mt. Carmel area of Palestine: Site catchment analysis. _Proceedings of the Prehistoric Society_ 36:1-37.

Jochim, M. A.
1976 _Hunter Gatherer Subsistence and Settlement: A Predictive Model._ New York: Academic Press.

Johnson, E.
1983 A framework of interpretation in bone technology. In _Carnivores, Human Scavengers and Predators: A Question of Bone Technology_, edited by G. M. LeMoine and A. S. MacEachern, pp. 55-93. Calgary: University of Calgary Archaeological Association.

Jones, K. T.
1983 Forager archaeology: The Aché of Eastern Paraguay. In _Carnivores, Human Scavengers and Predators: A Question of Bone Technology_, edited by G. M. LeMoine and A. S. MacEachern, pp. 171-191. Calgary: University of Calgary Archaeological Association.

Kelley, J. H.
1966 _The Archaeology of the Sierra Blanca Region of Southeastern New Mexico._ Unpublished Ph.D. Dissertation. Cambridge: Harvard University.

1979 The Sierra Blanca restudy project. In _Jornada Mogollon Archaeology_, edited by P. H. Beckett and R. N. Wiseman, pp. 107-122. Las Cruces: New Mexico State University.

1984 _The Archaeology of the Sierra Blanca Region of Southeastern New Mexico._ Anthropological Paper 74. Ann Arbor: University of Michigan Museum of Anthropology.

Kooyman, B.
n.d. A faunal analysis of two New Mexican pueblo sites. Manuscript on file, Department of Archaeology, University of Calgary, Calgary.

Korth, W. W.
1979 Taphonomy of microvertebrate fossil assemblages. _Annals of the Carnegie Museum_ 48:235-285.

Lawrence, B.
1951 _Postcranial Skeletal Characteristics of Deer, Pronghorn, and Sheep-Goat, with Notes on Bos and Bison._ Papers of the Peabody Museum of American Archaeology and Ethnology XXXV(3), Part II. Cambridge: Harvard University.

Lewall, E. E., and I. M. Cowan
1963 Age determination in blacktail deer by degree of ossification of the epiphyseal plate in the long bones. Canadian Journal of Zoology 41(4):629-636.

Lowe, V. P. W.
1980 Variation in digestion of prey by the Tawny Owl (Strix aluco). Journal of the Zoological Society of London 192:283-293.

Maher, L. J.
1972 Absolute pollen diagram of Redrock Lake, Boulder County, Colorado. Quaternary Research 2:531-553.

Maltby, M.
1979 Faunal Studies on Urban Sites: the Animal Bones from Exeter 1971-1975. Exeter Archaeological Reports 2. Sheffield: University of Sheffield.

1982 The variability of faunal samples and their effects upon ageing data. In Ageing and Sexing Animal Bones from Archaeological Sites, edited by B. Wilson, C. Grigson, and S. Payne, pp. 81-90. British Series 109. Oxford: British Archaeological Reports.

Meadow, R. H.
1978 Effects of context on the interpretation of faunal remains: A case study. In Approaches to Faunal Analysis in the Middle East, edited by R. H. Meadow and M. A. Zeder, pp. 15-21. Peabody Museum Bulletin 2. Cambridge: Harvard University.

Nimmo, B. W.
1971 Population dynamics of a Wyoming pronghorn cohort from the Eden-Farson site, 48SW304. Plains Anthropologist 16(54):285-288.

Olsen, S. J.
1964 Mammal Remains from Archaeological Sites, Part 1: Southeastern and Southwestern United States. Papers of the Peabody Museum of American Archaeology and Ethnology 56(1). Cambridge: Harvard University.

Perkins, D., and P. Daly
1968 A hunters' village in Neolithic Turkey. Scientific American 219:97-106.

Raish, C., A. Earls, J. Wilson, and L. Cordell
1984 Depositional patterns in cobble/adobe rooms: A case study from the Rio Grande. In Recent Research in Mogollon Archaeology, edited by S. Upham, F. Plog, D. G. Batcho, and B. E. Kauffman, pp. 115-124. Occasional Paper 10. Las Cruces: University Museum, New Mexico State University.

Shotwell, J. A.
1955 An approach to the paleoecology of mammals. Ecology 36:327-337.

Silver, I. A.
1969 The ageing of domestic animals. In Science in Archaeology, edited by D. R. Brothwell and E. S. Higgs, pp. 283-302. London: Thames and Hudson.

Speth, J. D.
1983 Bison Kills and Bone Counts. Chicago: University of Chicago Press.

Speth, J. D., and S. Scott
1983 Late prehistoric subsistence change in southeastern New Mexico: The faunal evidence from the Sacramentos. Paper presented at the Third Jornada Mogollon Conference, El Paso, Texas, October 1983.

1984 The role of large mammals in late prehistoric horticultural adaptations: The view from southeastern New Mexico. Paper presented to the 17th Annual Meeting, Canadian Archaeological Association, Victoria, B.C., April 1984.

1985 The role of large mammals in late prehistoric horticultural adaptations: The view from southeastern New Mexico. In Contributions to Plains Prehistory: The 1984 Victoria Symposium, edited by D. V. Burley. Occasional Paper 26. Edmonton: Archaeological Survey of Alberta.

Speth, J. D., and K. A. Spielmann
1983 Energy source, protein metabolism and hunter-gatherer subsistence strategies. Journal of Anthropological Archaeology 2:1-31.

Spielmann, K. A.
1983 Late prehistoric exchange between the Southwest and the Southern Plains. Plains Anthropologist 28(102):257-272.

Thomas, D. H.
1971 On distinguishing natural from cultural bone in archaeological sites. American Antiquity 36:366-371.

Thomson, H. P., and O. A. Mortenson
1946 Bone growth as an age criterion in the cottontail rabbit. Journal of Wildlife Management 10(2):171-174.

Tyler, H. A.
1964 Pueblo Animals and Myths. Norman: University of Oklahoma Press.

Vigne, J.-D., and M.-C. Marinval-Vigne
1983 Methode pour la mise en evidence de la consommation du petit gibier. In Animals and Archaeology: 1. Hunters and their Prey, edited by J. Clutton-Brock and C. Grigson, pp. 239-242. International Series 163. Oxford: British Archaeological Reports.

Watson, J. P. N.
1978 The interpretation of epiphyseal fusion data. In Research Problems in Zooarchaeology, edited by D. R. Brothwell, K. D. Thomas, and J. Clutton-Brock, pp. 97-101. Occasional Publication 3. London: Institute of Archaeology.

1979 The estimation of the relative frequencies of mammalian species: Khirokitia 1972. Journal of Archaeological Science 6:127-137.

White, T. E.
1952 Observations on the butchery technique of some aboriginal peoples, 1. American Antiquity 17(4):337-338.

Winterhalder, B., and E. A. Smith (eds.)
1981 Hunter-gatherer Foraging Strategies. Chicago: University of Chicago Press.

Wiseman, R. N.
1983 Archaeological taxonomy and confusion--welcome to the Jornada! COAS: New Mexico Archaeology and History 1(1):17-26.

1984 Ceramics from the Garnsey Spring Campsite. In The Garnsey Spring Campsite: Late Prehistoric Occupation in Southeastern New Mexico, by W. J. Parry and J. D. Speth, pp. 73-83. Technical Report 15. Ann Arbor: University of Michigan Museum of Anthropology.

Young, G.
1980 Analysis of faunal remains. In Tijeras Canyon: Analyses of the Past, edited by L. S. Cordell, pp. 88-120. Albuquerque: University of New Mexico Press.